CONTINENTAL EUROPE

Country Inns and Back Roads

Including some castles, pensions,
country houses, chateaux, farmhouses, palaces,
traditional inns, chalets, villas,
and small hotels.

**By Norman T. Simpson
The Berkshire Traveller**

A Harper Colophon Book

1817

HARPER & ROW, PUBLISHERS, New York
Cambridge, Philadelphia, San Francisco,
London, Mexico City, São Paulo, Singapore, Sydney

TRAVEL BOOKS BY NORMAN T. SIMPSON

Country Inns and Back Roads, North America
Country Inns and Back Roads, Britain and Ireland
Country Inns and Back Roads, Continental Europe
Bed and Breakfast, American Style

COVER PAINTING: Scene in Eze, France, by anonymous street artist
DRAWINGS: Janice Lindstrom

COUNTRY INNS AND BACK ROADS, CONTINENTAL EUROPE. Copyright © 1985 by
Harper & Row Publishers, Inc. All rights reserved. Printed in the United States of
America. No part of this book may be used or reproduced in any manner whatsoever
without written permission except in the case of brief quotations embodied in critical
articles and reviews. For information address Harper & Row, Publishers, Inc., 10 East
53rd Street, New York, N.Y. 10022. Published simultaneously in Canada by Fitzhenry &
Whiteside Limited, Toronto.

First HARPER COLOPHON edition.

Library of Congress Cataloging in Publication Data

Simpson, Norman T.
    Country inns and back roads.

    (A Harper colophon book)
    Includes index.
    1. Hotels, taverns, etc.—Europe—Directories.
I. Title.
TX910.A1S55   1985   647'.94401   84-48625
ISBN 0-06-091243-X (pbk.)

85 86 87 88 89 HC 10 9 8 7 6 5 4 3 2 1

CONTENTS

"The earth is the Lord's, and the fullness thereof; the world, and they that dwell therein."

Psalm 24

INTRODUCTION

The first printing of this book in 1976 had one outstanding virtue: the introduction lasted only one page. However, subsequent revisions, expansions, and travel have provided me with a growing overview, and so in this edition the introduction will probably run a bit longer.

Now, a few explanations and disclaimers: this book is not intended as a one-volume, overall guide to the countries of Europe. Rather, it is my adventures on a series of itineraries. My main purpose is to encourage travel in any form, although for the most part it is ideally suited for use by two or four people using an automobile. Travelers can follow my suggested itineraries or branch out for themselves, particularly at times other than the high season. I encourage my readers to feel free to move about with maps, guides, and a light heart, expecting the best because they will find it. Basically, the good people of the countries included herein are courteous and helpful, and the accounts of my experiences are liberally sprinkled with how I was aided by many individuals. I do not speak any foreign languages well, although I rapidly learned to communicate wherever I went.

Renting a Car for Europe

For many years I have made all of my automobile renting arrangements through AutoEurope. Through them I found I could pick up a car in one country and leave it in another, and there are AutoEurope agencies available in every one of the countries covered in this volume. The toll-free AutoEurope number in the U.S.A. is 1-800-223-5555 (from New York State, call 1-800-942-1309). I have always found their service very satisfactory.

Traveling to Europe

I heartily recommend a visit to your travel agent for unraveling the tremendously intricate special fares that seem to be undergoing constant changes these days. A travel agent can be very useful in simplifying the myriad details by making advance reservations for most of the inns in this book. The travel agent receives a commission from many of the accommodations, but where this is not true, you should expect to pay a reasonable reservation fee for the handling of such details.

Incidentally, a Eurail pass can be purchased only in the United States.

Everybody has favorite airlines, and for some years I've had a very warm place in my heart for Pan American. I've flown almost everywhere in Europe on this veteran airline. It has always worked well for me.

Rates

The rates vary, with an emphasis on the upper middle range. All the rates are in the Index, and these are changed, as necessary, in subsequent reprintings so that they should be fairly current.

The rates quoted in this book are meant as guidelines only. Basically, they are the cost of one night's lodging for two people, and many times include a continental breakfast. Most of the time they are quoted in the money of the country involved; however, in some cases, it was necessary to give the cost in American dollars. Please bear in mind that the rates listed are designed only to give the reader a general idea.

A Few Final Words

If you have been waiting to visit Europe until after the kids are out of college or a new roof has been put on the house, don't wait—go now. It is an absolutely fantastic experience. But for goodness' sake, don't try to do too much in one trip.

No one knows how long the U.S. dollar will be so strong against foreign currency, but it certainly makes a strong case for visiting abroad in the foreseeable future.

I carry tape recorders, not only to record all of my impressions (you should do the same because they match up extremely well with photographs), but also to play cassette tapes of the music of the various countries. Imagine listening to Grieg's *Norwegian Dances* while traveling the fjords of Norway; the *Suite Espanola* of Albéniz while high in the mountains of Spain; Ravel in Paris and Mozart in Vienna!

Send me at least one postcard: Norman Simpson, Stockbridge, MA 01262. I love to hear from people who are using my books for traveling in Europe.

Pack under the assumption that you are going to have to carry all the bags yourself. Personally, I only take carry-on luggage and do a small laundry every night.

Don't bother to learn twelve new languages, but at least be able to say "Please" and "Thank You," wherever you may go.

I found I could use my Visa credit card almost everywhere. American Express is also widely used.

For many years I've had an extensive correspondence with the places mentioned in this book. These European innkeepers love it when you show them a copy of *CIBR, Continental Europe*, and it is a good opportunity for you to give them my personal best wishes.

A Word of Thanks

This is an opportunity to express thanks to Elisabeth Szigeti for her good advice and research on not only Paris and some of the country chateaux of France, but also on places in Italy, Switzerland, and Hungary.

INNS and LOCATION

Germany

• PARIS
  • Barbizon
    • Les Blezards

• AVALLON

EASTERN FRANCE

ITINERARY # 1 (Page 17)

•Vonnas

•LYON

Condrieu•

St-Romain-de-Lerps •

Baix •

Rhone Valley

•AVIGNON

Noves •

Trigance •

Tourtour •

MARSEILLE

Vence •

Eze Village •

•Roquebrune

NICE

•Cagnes-sur Mer'

•St. Tropez

• Nans-les-Pins

Italy

11

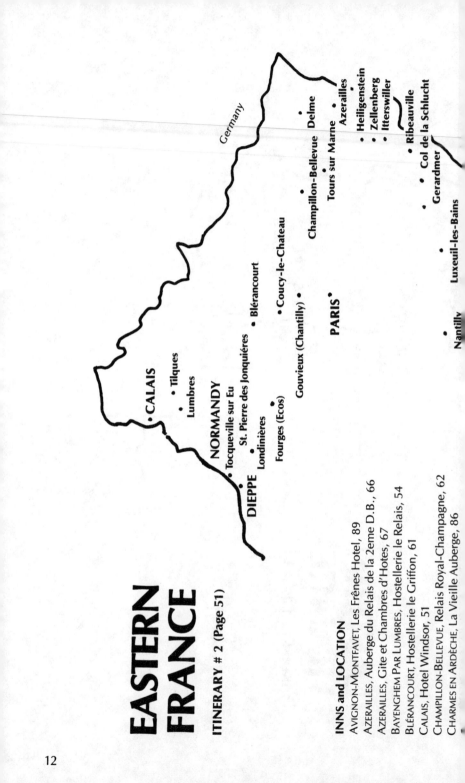

EASTERN FRANCE

ITINERARY # 2 (Page 51)

Germany

NORMANDY

CALAIS

Tilques
• Lumbres

Tocqueville sur Eu
St. Pierre des Jonquiéres
• Blérancourt
DIEPPE
Londinières
Fourges (Ecos)
• Coucy-le-Chateau

Gouvieux (Chantilly) •

• Champillon-Bellevue   • Delme
Tours sur Marne   • Azerailles
• Heiligenstein
• Zellenberg
• Itterswiller
• Ribeauville
• Col de la Schlucht
• Gerardmer

PARIS •

• Luxeuil-les-Bains

• Nantilly

INNS and LOCATION

AVIGNON-MONTFAVET, Les Frênes Hotel, 89

AZERAILLES, Auberge du Relais de la 2eme D.B., 66

AZERAILLES, Gite et Chambres d'Hotes, 67

BAYENGHEM PAR LUMBRES, Hostellerie le Relais, 54

BLÉRANCOURT, Hostellerie le Griffon, 61

CALAIS, Hotel Windsor, 51

CHAMPILLON-BELLEVUE, Relais Royal-Champagne, 62

CHARMES EN ARDÈCHE, La Vieille Auberge, 86

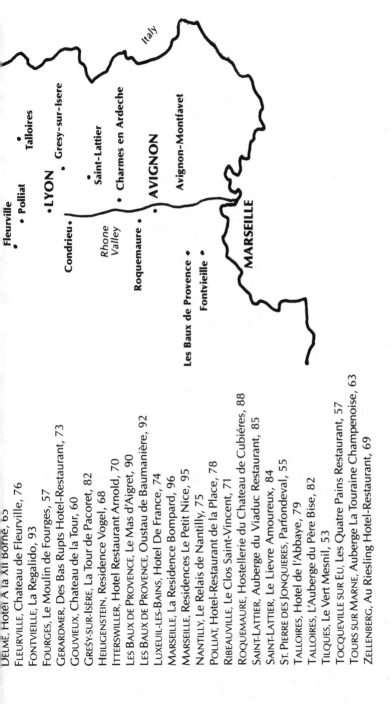

Italy

Fleurville
• Polliat
• Talloires

•LYON
Gresy-sur-Isere

Condrieu•
Saint-Lattier
• Charmes en Ardeche

Rhone
Valley
• AVIGNON
Roquemaure •
Avignon-Montfavet

MARSEILLE

Les Baux de Provence •
Fontvieille •

13

TRAVEL SUGGESTIONS FOR FRANCE

How to Get There

Pan Am, Air France, and many other airlines fly directly from North America to Paris. Your travel agent is your best source for expert opinion about the many different packages and constantly-changing special fares offered by many airlines. A Eurailpass is good in France.

Country Inns in France

The accommodations I visited are as diversified and complex as the country itself. They are located in ancient castles, chateaux, country houses, priories, conventional small and large hotels, and private homes. The price range is also very wide. In some cases, I splurged one night and became very economical the following night. There is a long tradition of personal innkeeping in France; in most cases, the proprietors themselves make their guests feel very much at home.

Bed and breakfast has never been very popular in France, but the idea was picked up recently by two different organizations. It is now possible to find accommodations both with farmers and castle owners (who are sometimes farmers themselves). For rooms on a farm, ask the Syndicat d' Initiative (local tourist bureau); for rooms at private chateaux, contact Bertrand Laffilé at the Demeures Club, 5 Place du Marché Sainte Catherine, 75004 Paris, France. For a further description of this venture see the section on Normandy.

Reservations

You and your travel agent can contact by telephone, either from North America or from France, every one of the accommodations mentioned in this book. You can travel either by a set itinerary or take it from night-to-night. I've done both and I don't speak acceptable French. I encourage adventuresome North Americans to travel to France in the off-season and try a few days of unscheduled travel. Every French tourist office in every city can make reservations, not only for local lodgings but also for those in other localities, through all other tourist offices in France.

Regardless of price, most of the accommodations I visited were clean and basically acceptable. I took quite a few sight-unseen. A traveler can have an absolutely marvelous experience in France by staying at accommodations that are members of the Relais de Campagne Chateaux-Hotels, an organization dedicated to the highest innkeeping standards. I have noted several in this book in both of my major itineraries as well as in Paris. These accommodations are in castles, chateaux, country houses, and the like, and you can make reservations by contacting: David Mitchell & Company, (212) 696-1323. Reservations and confirmation can be made very easily for all of the member hotels, including those in other countries. Incidentally, at most hotels in France, breakfast is additional and in some cases a service charge is added. The rates that are included in the Index are for two people for one night.

For Itinerary Number One (Paris south to the Riviera), I had everything reserved in advance. For Itinerary Number Two (Calais across northern France to the Rhine River and back through the French Alps; on to the Rhone River and south to Bordeaux), I made reservations a day in advance. Both systems worked beautifully.

Car Rentals

You can rent a car at almost every railroad station and airport in France. You can also make reservations for your car to be picked up at one point and dropped at another anywhere in France or Europe. See the section near the front of this book, "Renting a Car for Europe."

Driving in France

Let's begin with Paris. Like all of the principal cities of Europe and America, Paris has lots of traffic—but not as bad as I expected. While driving my rented car, I discovered that the drivers on the whole were quite courteous and the problem looks a lot worse than it is. You simply have to plunge in to discover that the traffic through the Arc de Triomphe is quite manageable. I hit it on my very first day in Paris and it was raining cats and dogs.

The beltway around Paris, called the Periphique, has roads leading from it in all directions. The best thing to do when leaving Paris is to identify carefully both the number and the names of the principal cities on your route, such as Orleans, Chartres, or Lyon. Study the Michelin map in advance and exit the Periphique at roads leading to the main city on your route.

Country driving in France is like country driving anywhere else. You'll probably discover that the French drive a great deal faster than the USA's 55-m.p.h.-speed limit. If they give you a dirty look as they whiz by just give them a friendly wave.

French Menus

I am not a gourmet in any sense of the word, and I don't consider myself an expert on food. Furthermore, my perusal of guides to French cuisine with the star ratings made me quite apprehensive about displaying my ignorance to French waiters and headwaiters. To top it all off, I really don't know anything about wines, except it is red wine for meat and white wine for fish. However, in all of the restaurants, brasseries, auberges, snack bars, bistros, and cafés I visited, I was treated with courtesy and consideration. I was surprised at how quickly I picked up "menu French."

In the French restaurants there are usually three fixed-price (prix fixe) menus. The higher the price, the wider the choice of the main dishes.

The à la carte menu has several advantages; for one thing, it is possible to skip a course or two and concentrate on something special. I quickly learned that ordering only soup (potage), bread (pain), salads, desserts, or cheese would not evoke any raised eyebrows or disdainful glances. There are over 400 different varieties of cheese in France, made from goat's, cow's, and ewe's milk. Sometimes several cheeses are served from a large tray and the diner can make a choice.

I encourage everyone going to France to put aside their preconceived notions about French cuisine and service. It is a delightful education and, if approached with an open mind and a carefree heart, can be a delightful experience. Enjoy.

Itineraries in France

This book is made up of two itineraries. One starts in Paris and goes south through the edge of Burgundy and continues on to the wine country at Beaune, following the Rhone River to Avignon, and then swings east to Provence and the Riviera. The second itinerary begins in Calais and pretty much wanders across northern France to the Rhine valley and then continues somewhat hit or miss back towards the center of France, but also includes a touch of the French Alps. The two itineraries run parallel for a few miles along the Rhone River, but then the second one branches off into the Camargue and Bordeaux.

Itinerary Number One—Paris-Nice

As I mentioned earlier, this is the first of two itineraries and most countryside accommodations are at members of the Relais et Chateaux and can be made through David Mitchell, (212) 696-1323. Call the Paris hotels directly.

Paris: Some Tips

The first important thing to know about Paris is that it is divided by the Seine River into two essentially distinct parts: the Right Bank to the north, and the Left Bank to the south. The Right Bank is conservative; the Left Bank swings. This distinction dates back to the old days. At the beginning of the century the "in" crowd, consisting as always of artists and writers, used to hang around Montmartre. But, in the thirties, this changed when everybody moved down to Montparnasse. Then, in the forties, the crowd settled in the area of Saint Germain, named after the church of Saint Germain des Prés, and the existentialists gathered around Jean-Paul Sartre at the "Rhumerie," one of the cafés on the Boulevard Saint Germain. At night, everyone went into the caves (cellars) or the boites (boxes), two French names for nightclubs, and danced to the sound of jazz. Ever since, the Left Bank is "in" and the Right Bank, "out."

Most of the interesting sights, though, are in a very central area, easy to get to on the subway. The Parisian "metro" is reliable, comfortable and fast; it is also simple to use. The bus system is also very convenient and clear route maps are posted at each bus stop.

The R.A.T.P. (this is the name of the public company that runs the bus and subway systems in Paris) offers special tourist tickets: two-, four-, and seven-day packages. With these tickets you can ride endlessly on the bus or the metro (in first class). And if you like to plan ahead, you may purchase these special tickets from the offices of S.N.C.F. (the French railroad system) in New York, San Francisco, Chicago, Los Angeles, and Miami.

Any problem concerning your trip in France (tours, visits, hotels) can probably be solved by the Office du Tourisme de Paris. Go to the head office on the Champs Elysées, number 127, or to the other offices in the railway stations or at the Tour Eiffel. They are open every day of the week from 9 a.m. to 10 p.m., and on Sundays and public holidays from 9 a.m. to 8 p.m.

Paris on the Bus

If you don't feel like taking a guided bus tour you can easily get a first contact with the city on your own on the public bus. Start at the Place de l'Opéra. At the top of the Avenue de l'Opéra, which goes south from the bottom of the Opéra Square in front of the Opéra itself, is a bus stop. Climb into number 81, 27, or 21 to "Chatelet." Tell the driver to let you know your stop. It is a pretty route, down the avenue and then alongside the Louvre Museum and the Seine River.

At "Chatelet," the name of one of the two theaters facing each other on this square, cross the river on foot to the Ile de la Cité. You may choose to walk to the Cathedral of Notre Dame through the flower market; it is a five-minute walk. You can also visit the Sainte Chapelle in the Palace of Justice, the church of Saint Louis.

In front of the Palace of Justice, take any bus and get off at "Les Ecoles." This is the heart of the "Latin Quarter" and you are in front of Musée de Cluny. At the corner of Rue des Ecoles and Boulevard Saint Michel, take bus number 63. It goes to Saint Germain des Prés, an interesting church, and also the name of the neighborhood where the existentialists gathered around Jean-Paul Sartre after the war. Then on to the Invalides on the same bus, where you may choose to see Napoleon's grave.

Behind the Invalides compound on Avenue de Tourville is the stop for bus 82, which will take you to the Tour Eiffel. Then, crossing *the river and the gardens of Trocadero, arrive at the start of Avenue Kleber, where you will find bus Number 30 to take you to the Arc de Triomphe (Etoile).*

From there you can either walk down the Champs Elysées to the Place de la Concorde or take bus Number 73.

If you visit only one place thoroughly and don't linger too long elsewhere, this being only a reconnoitering trip, you may arrive at Concorde in time for lunch at Maxim's.

HÔTEL DE CRILLON, Paris

I daresay that most of the North American travelers in France will fly directly to Paris. With this in mind, I have included some small Parisian hotels of varying price ranges and locations. Since there are at least three hotels in the luxury class in Paris, I thought it would be fun to include one of them, just as I have with the Ritz in Madrid.

I chose the Hôtel de Crillon, centrally located in a most desirable location overlooking Place de la Concorde, with the Tuileries and the Louvre to the left, and the U.S. Embassy and the Champs-Elysées to the right.

For one thing, it doesn't look like a hotel. It resembles one of the elegant public buildings of Paris, many of which were former palaces, as is the case here; 1758 is one of the dates that sticks in my mind. It's been a hotel more than a hundred years.

Today, affluent guests can enjoy the 180 bedrooms and 30 suites, as well as the cuisine.

I have visited the Hôtel de Crillon on two occasions, separated by a year, and each time I was shown about by the voluble and attractive Michèle de la Clergerie, who is in charge of public relations for the hotel. On the occasion of the first visit, the central courtyard was being completely rehabilitated, plans were made for redecorating and redesigning many of the famous *salons* and many of the bedrooms and apartments were undergoing great changes.

A year later, most of this work had been completed and, in fact, on the day of my visit the newly decorated and designed center courtyard was the scene of a photographic session with the chef and members of his staff arrayed in brilliant white uniforms and hats.

Michèle de la Clergerie explained that all the accommodations had been furnished with new bathrooms and many had soundproofing, air conditioning, radio, and TV sets. "We have made a great deal of progress," she said. "But we still have a few more things to accomplish, including the creation of the gallery-sitting room that will be a link between the lobby and the restaurant."

The experience at Hôtel de Crillon is one of Continental luxury. The facade is relatively conservative, but the lobby and public rooms are sumptuously decorated as only the French can do it, with elaborate and detailed paintings on walls and ceilings and polished marble floors.

HÔTEL DE CRILLON (Relais et Chateaux), 10 Place de la Concorde, 75008 Paris. Tel.: 296-10-81. (U.S.A. reservations: 800-223-6800.) (New York State: 212-838-3110 collect.) Rates: See Index.

Directions: Take a cab or the airport bus from either Orly or De Gaulle Airports.

LA RESIDENCE DU BOIS, Paris

There I was, spread out at my own circular table with a red tablecloth, enjoying the perfect lunch at La Residence du Bois. Momentarily alone in the garden of this exquisite little hotel, I really felt as if I had discovered one of the few quiet places of Paris, even though some of the adjacent buildings looked down upon this tiny enclave. The birds fluttered down to seek some crumbs and other tidbits from other tables, and the trees, now in full leaf, acted as a protection against the midday sun.

The waiter materialized from the miniature forest with a wonderful platter of meats and cheeses, a heaping bowl of lettuce greens with just the right mustard dressing, two fresh hard rolls, and a delicious glass of Perrier with lemon.

A morning in Paris walking along the Seine or touring the Louvre, or even venturing into the many gardens, can leave the traveler a little breathless and, during the warm season, not a little overheated. Having spent such a morning, I was now raising a glass in the direction of Oklahoma to Linda Lee Tharp for recommending this lovely little hotel. She assured me that it was exactly what I was trying to find in Paris: "The right touch of elegance, the right kind of attention and service without any obsequiousness."

I had already seen quite a few of the twenty bedrooms, all of which were notable for a restrained elegance and blessed quietness.

One of the pleasing features of La Residence du Bois has to be the wonderful concierge, who is a woman of great charm and limit-

less information. She explained that although breakfast is served to all houseguests, a simple lunch and dinner can also be obtained with a modest amount of notice. It's just the kind of service that I can appreciate because, although Paris can be a gastronomic adventure, there are times when all that is needed is a simple, quiet meal.

LA RESIDENCE DU BOIS (Relais et Chateaux), 16 rue Chalgrin, 75116 Paris. Tel.: 500-50-59. A 20-guestroom very quiet, comfortable, calm hotel in the 16th Arrondissement. Open year-round. Breakfast included in price of room. Simple lunches and dinners available on request to houseguests only. A few blocks from the Arc de Triomphe. A garage adjacent. Rates: See Index.

Directions: From Orly or De Gaulle airports, I suggest the airport bus and a taxi.

HÔTEL SAINT-SIMON, Paris

Turning off Boulevard Saint Germain and leaving behind the noise and tumult of pedestrian and automobile traffic, one finds rue Saint-Simon, a haven of provincial peace. Located in the heart of the Latin Quarter on the chic west side, the Hôtel Saint-Simon has a longstanding reputation for comfort and old-time elegance. In 1977, it passed into the hands of a very refined Swedish gentleman, Göran

Lindquist, who wanted to elevate the hotel to the four-star class. He cast a new spell on the establishment, adding an elevator, a breakfast room, a bar, and common room. He also redecorated all the rooms using very pretty fabrics and putting handmade tiles from the south of France in most bathrooms.

"But everything is simple, no chi-chis," he stresses. "One should feel in a friend's country home right here in the heart of Paris." He has achieved his goal admirably, especially since many of the rooms overlook a string of private gardens. Some even have their own terraces with flowers, a welcome addition in the summer.

Mme. Lalisse, the director of the hotel, explained that she gives special attention to breakfast, to her the most important meal in the day. Fresh orange juice is served (a real rarity anywhere), excellent coffee, and "real" *croissant au beurre*.

HOTEL SAINT-SIMON, 14 rue de Saint-Simon, 75007 Paris. Tel.: 548-35-66. A 34-guestroom, very comfortable hotel on a quiet street on the Left Bank. Place de la Concorde and the Louvre are within walking distance. No restaurant. Open all year. Rates: See Index.

Directions: From the airport or bus terminal, use a cab. During your stay, the metro station "rue du Bac" is very convenient.

HOTEL ESMERALDA, Paris

Across the Seine from Notre Dame is the Esmeralda Hotel. A small and lively woman, Michèle Bruel, is the manager. Michele loves the river, couldn't live without it. So, when she had to leave her apartment on the Ile Saint Louis, she looked around and found that a very small and very shabby hotel was offered for lease on rue Saint Julien le Pauvre, two steps away from the "quai." She grabbed it and found herself master of an establishment with about twenty-five rooms and only one bathroom. The hotel belonged to the lowest category, the type of place the police visit in the early hours to check on the occupants. It was a picturesque spot and still is, but now with new reasons.

The setting is still the same, an oblique narrow building facing the garden of the church of Saint Julien le Pauvre. But thanks to Michèle's excellent taste and obstinacy, the inside has become most attractive. The quaint little lobby is warm and welcoming, the rooms are airy and cozy, and many of them now have baths. The front rooms look over the garden and have a view of the river and Notre Dame.

A list of all the famous people who discovered the Esmeralda and stayed there would be endless, including Maurice Béjart and Terence Stamp. But there is more to this hotel—it is a place people come back to, and Michèle smiles while telling me about the little Esmeralda who came recently with her parents who had spent their honeymon at the hotel.

HOTEL ESMERALDA, 4 rue Saint Julien le Pauvre, 75005 Paris. Tel.: 325-37-32 or 354-19-20. A 19-guestroom hotel, two steps from Notre Dame and the Seine. Open all year. Rates: See Index.

Directions: From the airport or air terminal take a cab. Next subway station is "Saint Michel."

"L'HÔTEL," Paris

Staying at the "Hôtel" is like wearing an oversized gem. This explains why Liz Taylor likes it. But she's not the only one—most of the show business people coming to Paris stay there, too.

It's the place to go when one is bored with the Crillon or the Plaza Athénée, the two very best hotels in Paris. The "Hôtel" is the third "very best." A four-star deluxe hotel, it is really a grand hotel in miniature, offering everything a larger hotel of the same category can offer and one thing more: flair. This is a quality shared both by the creators of this extraordinary place and its guests.

Each room has its own decor and is furnished with genuine antiques. Some are really very special, like the room of Oscar Wilde, who died in the hotel in 1900, and the room of Mistinguett, who never stayed here, but whose private bedroom was reinstalled in a very authentic setting.

The "Hôtel" is located on the rue des Beaux Arts, a typical Left Bank street, especially on the days when the students of the nearby School of Architecture march out with their band and start a ball.

The day I visited there the owner, Guy Louis Duboucheron, was taking part in an antique airplane rally from Paris to Cannes. Don't expect to meet him, he's never there. But the staff is perfect. Staying at the "Hôtel" is better than being a guest in a friend's mansion—it's like "making yourself at home" while the host is away.

"L'HÔTEL," 13 rue des Beaux Arts, 75006 Paris. Tel.: 325-27-22. Telex 270-870. A 27-guestroom deluxe hotel on the Left Bank. Restaurant is closed in Aug., but the hotel is open all year. Rates vary with the size of the rooms, some of which are quite small and only have a shower (made of solid marble of course). Rates: See Index.

Directions: Taxi from the airport or bus terminal. During your stay you may use bus #95, which stops around the corner and goes toward Montparnasse in one direction and the Louvre and the Opera in the other.

※ ※ ※ ※

LES SEMAILLES RESTAURANT, Paris

A visit to this section, near the Champs-Elysées, should be planned ahead in order to include lunch or dinner in this excellent restaurant. René Salmon and Jean Jacques Jouteux ask that all reservations be confirmed on the morning of the chosen day. It is an expensive place, but if you go to the "tourist" restaurants it will cost you almost the same price and it will probably not be as pleasant an experience.

Les Semailles is a perfect place because Jean Jacques Jouteux is a born perfectionist and because he genuinely loves his work. He is one of those lucky people who never hesitated about what they wanted to do; he decided to become a cook when he was eleven years old. He started his apprenticeship at fourteen and then roamed about France to learn from other great cooks. He wandered for a long time before actually starting and really opening a restaurant.

One of the striking things is the way René Salmon welcomes his guests. It is as if you were really a guest, which in a way you are.

The menu (à la carte) changes four times a year and never repeats itself. Jean Jacques Jouteux is a learned cook with a very personal poetic touch. His plates resemble authentic *tableaux de maitre* (masterpieces). They are a pleasure for the eye as well as the palate. He calls it *haute cuisine* and it is.

LES SEMAILLES RESTAURANT, 34 rue de Colisée. Tel.: 256-1682. Really one of the few perfectly refined restaurants in Paris. Reserve long in advance, it is worth it. About 300 francs per person. Closed Sun. and Mon.

Having completed our tour of Paris, we now are ready to venture forth into the countryside from Paris to the Riviera. The first stop is about an hour and a half from Paris, off of Autoroute 86.

HOTELLERIE DU BAS-BREAU, Barbizon

I was having my first dinner in a French country inn, and to make it even more exciting, I was having my first genuine French soufflé. Its golden crust rose from the traditional white soufflé dish, proclaiming with a magnificent Gallic insouciance that it was, indeed, master of all it surveyed. For one breathless moment I was allowed to dwell on this model of perfection. Such style! Such grace! Such nobility! Such a divine fragrance!

The last, alas, was to be its undoing—I could wait no longer. And even while administering the *coupe de grace*, I realized that this *chef d'oeuvre* had withheld its crowning achievement to the very last moment. Closing my eyes to savor that first heavenly morsel, my senses thrilled to the indescribable taste of—praline soufflé!! I lost all touch with time and space . . . I was, indeed, on Olympus and this was ambrosia of the gods.

"You are, perhaps, enjoying your soufflé?" It was Jean-Pierre Fava, the innkeeper of du Bas-Breau, who stood beside my table with a twinkle in his eye. For a moment I could only nod vigorously, and then I regained my voice. "It is unlike anything I have ever tasted," I said.

"You are very kind," he replied. "And I am happy to say we receive many compliments for our praline soufflé."

One hundred and fifty years ago this inn on the edge of the Barbizon Forest carried on its signboard the name of its proprietor, M. Siron, and its best-known guest was Robert Louis Stevenson. The name was changed in 1867 to Hotel de l'Exposition, because it was being used as an exhibition hall for the Barbizon painters, including Corot, Rousseau, and Millet, all of whom painted in the forest. It became du Bas-Breau in 1937, when M. and Mme. Fava arrived, and its tradition, elegance, comfort, and gastronomy have since become well known. Jean-Pierre, the present innkeeper, is continuing the ideals of his parents.

The entrance to the inn is through an arch into a small courtyard with cobblestones and two big pots of geraniums and ivy. There are flowers everywhere, even in little flowerpots on the roof. An ancient French lamp hangs from the arch and a stairway leads up to some guest rooms with window boxes full of flowers.

The next entrance is into the main reception hall and bar, where *petit déjeuner* is served each morning. Through the windows I could see the dining courtyard and other buildings containing more guest rooms. In the evening, the scene is lit with discreet lanterns, and the tables are occupied with happy diners.

All of the bedrooms have triple sheets, handsome bedspreads, and show pillows; many of them overlook a terrace, and others provide a generous glimpse of the gardens of the village. During my visit, the fruit trees and lilacs were in vivid blossom.

As Jean-Pierre said, "Our guests enjoy walking in the Fontaine-bleau Forest, driving through the countryside, and spending hours in the local shops."

I will also add that I am sure they enjoy the praline soufflés.

HOTELLERIE DU BAS-BREAU (Relais et Chateaux), 77630 Barbizon. Tel.: (6) 066-40-05. A 19-guestroom exceptionally comfortable inn with first-class service on the edge of the Fontainebleau Forest, approx. 1½ hrs. south of Paris. Breakfast, lunch, dinner. Closed from Jan. 1 to Feb. 15. Rates: See Index.

Directions; Follow Autoroute A-6 (Michelin sect. map 61) marked Lyon to Fontainebleau. Use Exit (Sortie) for Barbizon.

AUBERGE DES TEMPLIERS, Les Bezards

Following Jean-Pierre Fava's directions, I left du Bas-Breau and Barbizon, and within a pleasant hour-and-a-half drive I pulled up at the great gates of the Auberge des Templiers. This is on the road southwest to the chateaux country.

I stepped through a heavy front door into the reception area and found a two-story room with a very impressive tapestry on the far wall. I moved into still another vaulted room with a replica of a Crusader's cross over the massive mantle.

An extremely attractive Frenchwoman with short, blonde hair, wearing a very chic striped grey and charcoal pantsuit, introduced herself, and she and I set out on a short tour of the many buildings and grounds. We walked across the garden, past the swimming pool and the barbecue lunch area. The tennis courts were just beyond. There were many trees and attractively landscaped lawns. We looked at several guest rooms and I found them beautifully furnished. "We are just a short, pleasant drive from Paris, so many of our Parisian guests come and stay a few days at a time," she said. "There is much to be seen and done all within automobiling distance."

At lunch I learned that this particular region of France sent many knights to the Crusades, and that this building at one time must have been an abbey and a meeting place for the men-at-arms who set off on the great adventure. The word "Templiers" actually refers to a certain order of Crusaders. I found many references to this historical event throughout southern France.

A beautiful inn, a congenial innkeeping family, tranquility and graciousness. I found these at Auberge des Templiers. It was like an American country inn with a French accent.

AUBERGE DES TEMPLIERS (Relais et Chateaux), 45290 Les Bezards. Tel.: (38) 31-80-01. A 25-guestroom exceptionally comfortable chateau-inn with first-class service 135 km. south of Paris. Breakfast, lunch, dinner. This is a resort accommodation with a swimming pool, two tennis courts, horseback riding, and golf nearby. Closed Jan. 15 to Feb. 15. Rates: See Index.

Directions: See Michelin sect. map 65. Exit A-6 at Dordives. Follow N-7 south to Les Bezards. If continuing into chateaux country (southwest), I advise Michelin 64, 68, and 72. (My line of direction in this book is almost due south.)

French Villages

I fell in love with the French villages . . . the old stone houses sometimes covered with stucco of all colors, depending upon local soil . . . the trees that had been there for centuries shading the squares and their outdoor tables and chairs . . . the churches, the small shops, and the ever-present fountain in the center of each village.

After a first trip to France, everyone has a favorite village, and it is great fun to go back and see if it has changed. Basically, of course, it never does. In the spring and fall, many villages are innundated with flowers . . . flowers in windows, in front yards, and in the square. Lucky, indeed, the traveler who arrives in the village on market day or even better when there is a carnival or a festival. It is a wonderful opportunity to see the villages in a holiday mood.

HOTEL LE CEP, Beaune

Hotel Le Cep is located in the heart of the town of Beaune, and I learned from Rosine Falci, the owner, that it is one of the richest wine towns in France. "People come from everywhere," she said, "to sample the burgundy wines at Beaune and many of them return to the hotel year after year.

Although no meals are offered here, there are many good restaurants nearby.

On my last visit, I noticed that guests in the sitting room were reading at the table or carrying on a conversation. It was quite informal—different from the more formal atmosphere that I found in other places. I unfolded my copy of the *Paris Herald Tribune* and caught up on things in the U.S.A.

The rooms in Le Cep are each decorated in the style of a different century of French architecture. Mine was in Louis XV.

Le Cep is a member of the Chateaux Hotels de France.

HOTEL LE CEP, 21200 Beaune. Tel.: (80) 22-35-48. A 20-guestroom in-town, comfortable but simple hotel in the Burgundy wine district, 37 km. south of Dijon. Member: Chateaux Hotels de France. Beaune is an extremely interesting and prosperous town with a great deal of emphasis on the surrounding vineyards. Closed Dec. 1 to Feb. 1. Rates: See Index.

Directions: Michelin sect. map 65. Follow one-way road circling the inside of the city about ¾ of the way around. Look for hotel sign on left. There is an exit at Beaune from Autoroute A-6.

CHATEAU D'IGE, Ige

"We are," said Monsieur Jadot, "very quiet." I was visiting my first ancient chateau hotel and I liked it immediately. This was enhanced by the smiling M. Jadot, who was the very personification of innkeeping joviality. It was obvious that he, too, was much attached to this 13th-century fortified home in the Burgundian countryside that seemed so far away from the demands of the 20th century.

First, we walked around the outside of the chateau, where the massive walls are overgrown with a green cloak of ivy. In the gardens a deep pool has been created by the waters of the brook, which was shared by playful ducks and unusually large trout. "The trout are too large for the ducks," said M. Jadot. There was a little outdoor dining terrace, which he explained was used for dinner in the warm weather. His German shepherd, Puff, walked ahead of us. Overhead, the sky was blue, the spring birds were singing, and some of the flowers were in bloom. It was, to say the least, idyllic. In one corner of the garden there was a tower with a most pleasant apartment. "Very popular with honeymooners," he said. The bedroom window on the top floor had a beautiful view of the village and the valley.

Inside the main building were several apartments, many of them also in the towers, reached by well-worn stone steps twisting around a center pole. Bedrooms were varied in size and looked comfortable.

This chateau had many, many old tapestries, which relieved the

rough texture of the grey-yellow stone walls. The furniture in the living and dining rooms was massive in style, and appropriate to the scale of the rooms.

Throughout my entire tour, Monsieur Jadot was smiling and laughing. We found several words in French and English that we shared in common.

Dinner is served only to houseguests and there is a choice of five main dishes. "We have a very good chef," he promised.

Chateau d'Ige was small by comparison to other castles I was to visit, but it had an undeniable warmth. I am sure its quiet atmosphere brings joy and happiness to many guests.

CHATEAU D'IGE (Relais et Chateaux), 71960 Ige. Tel.: (85) 33-33-99. A 9-guestroom, very comfortable 13th-century fortified chateau enhanced with modern conveniences. Approx. 80 km. north of Lyon. Breakfast and dinner served to houseguests only. Romantic countryside, golf, horseback riding, and sailing nearby. Closed Nov. 5 to Feb. 1. Rates: See Index.

Directions: Michelin sect. map 69, 73. Exit A-6 at Macon Nord and from Macon follow road marked Charolles. A few km. out of Macon turn right at the village of Vineuse (D-85). Follow road to Ige and inquire for inn.

LA MERE BLANC, Vonnas

It was high noon in Vonnas. The atmosphere and general spirit at La Mere Blanc was busy and cheerful. Waiters and waitresses were hustling and bustling back and forth, serving a large luncheon party in one dining room. My table next to the window overlooked a small stream. In the summertime meals are served on the terrace.

The proprietors are Jacqueline and Georges Blanc, third generation innkeepers. I was rather surprised because Georges didn't look more than twenty-five years old.

The youthful Monsieur Blanc explained that most of the items on the menu were regional specialties and that the menu included six courses. This was the meal that the French eat once a day, either at noon or night.

At his suggestion I ordered the creamed chicken with crêpes that, as he said, "enjoys a local reputation." I've had chicken in various garb all over the world, but I am sure that any chicken would consider it a noble sacrifice to be placed on the table at La Mere Blanc bathed in that truly marvelous cream sauce.

It was, however, the cream cheese that made this visit outstanding. I have never tasted such delicious, creamy, honestly-melt-in-the-mouth *fromage*. I ate every bit of it and as a result had to pass up the selection of six desserts.

There are several rooms in this small inn, all of them exceptionally well furnished and many with some rather startling color schemes, including lavender. Some of them had a kind of Spanish feeling about them.

Since my first visit, La Mere Blanc has become one of the most prestigious restaurants in France, the recipient of many accolades—more reason to take the short drive from the main Autoroute at Macon.

LA MERE BLANC (Relais et Chateaux), 01540 Vonnas. Tel.: (74) 50-00-10. An 18-guestroom very comfortable hotel with an excellent reputation for food. Breakfast, lunch, dinner. Swimming pool on grounds. Tennis, golf, horseback riding, fishing, nearby. Closed Dec. and Jan. Rates: See Index.

Directions: Michelin sect. map 91. Exit A-6 at Macon (Nord), follow N-79 approx. 10 km. on road to Bourg. Turn right at sign for Vonnas. La Mere Blanc is near the town square.

HOTELLERIE BEAU RIVAGE ET
L'HERMITAGE DU RHONE, Condrieu

I had been in France a few days and was feeling quite comfortable with my growing list of French verbs and nouns, when I arrived at Beau Rivage and immediately met another American couple who were on a combination business and pleasure trip. Since they were experienced travelers in France, I asked the husband for his opinion of French innkeeping. This is part of what he said:

"I have traveled in France several times and I have always found the French hotel keepers and their staff extremely accommodating and pleasant, and willing to go to any length to make their guests as comfortable as possible. For example, here, Madame Castaing has been the principal chef for many years, as well as being the owner, and you can see for yourself that she comes out of the kitchen frequently, exchanges a few words of conversation with her guests and radiates the feeling of hospitality."

Beau Rivage is right on the banks of the fast-flowing Rhone River as it makes its way south toward the Mediterranean. In the summertime, guests are served on patios overlooking the river and many of the guest rooms have a river view.

In addition to the extensive à la carte menu, there are also three set menus. I chose the middle one that included a delicious freshwater fish served in a very tasty sauce, succulent fresh French beans,

and a choice of three main dishes—steak, guinea hen, and lamb chops. There were also scalloped potatoes discreetly seasoned with garlic.

The headwaiter held a lively discussion with my friends about the features that lovers of good wine seem to hold so dear: the year, the fragrance, the length of time in the bottle, and even the name of the wine grower. "Yes, we French really do get down to the fine points of wine," he said. "The length of time the sun shines on the grapes during the day can play an important role, so that the exposure of the vineyards could be a factor." It was explained to me that wine grapes are gathered in late September because they cannot be picked in the rain.

I learned that many people stayed at Beau Rivage for several days at a time, because there is good fishing, horseback riding, tennis, golf, and the beautiful back roads of the incomparable countryside.

The evening was a marvelous success. Madame paid us a short visit and we toasted her dinner and her beautiful inn. Then we all resolved to sell our stocks and bonds and move to the Rhone Valley of France where we could meet frequently for dinner at Beau Rivage.

HOTELLERIE BEAU RIVAGE ET L'HERMITAGE DU RHONE (Relais et Chateaux), 69420 Condrieu. Tel.: (74) 59-52-24. A 25-guestroom very comfortable inn on the banks of the Rhone River, 60 km. south of Lyon. Breakfast, lunch, dinner. Tennis, swimming, golf, outdoor sports nearby. Closed early Jan. to middle Feb. Rates: See Index.

Directions: Michelin sect. map 93. As nearly as I can determine A-6 goes into A-7 at Lyon. Follow the road clearly marked Marseille and use the exit (Sortie) marked Condrieu. Proceed south on N-86 about 10 km. The inn is on the left between the road and the river.

South from Condrieu

It was Saturday morning along the Rhone. All the people from the little riverside villages were making a holiday of it, visiting the shops and stopping in the town square to exchange some tidbits of conversation with their friends. There were long loaves of delicious French bread carried under arms and colorful shopping bags loaded to the brim.

The towns and cities on the opposite side of the river were a picturebook sight with green vineyards and flower-laden orchards blending into the red roofs.

Following N-86 I could occasionally see the remains of an old tower or castle in the distance.

I turned off at St. Paray, en route to St. Romain-de-Lerps and had my first experience with high hills in France. As the road swung back and forth across little valleys and up into the higher ground, there were increasingly interesting panoramic views of the Rhone Valley. Since it was a promising May day with a warm sun, the industrious French farmers and their families were already working in the fields. To the south and east it was sunny, but the clouds and fog still had to burn off to the west.

Now, I had reached the village located at the crest of the hills and followed the signs over the rolling Burgundy countryside to Chateau du Besset.

LE CHATEAU DU BESSET, St.-Romain-de-Lerps

Sitting in the parlor of this 15th-century castle, I needed only court musicians playing Vivaldi or Bach to transport me to France before the Reign of Terror. Here were the casement windows, heavily beamed ceilings, rich furniture, tapestries, oils, and acquisitions from several epochs of French decoration and design that provided a clue as to how French royalty might have lived 200 years ago.

From one window I could look out over the fields and down into the valley to the green parkland, an essential feature of many French chateaux. Another window gave me an excellent view of the formal gardens where, with the encouragement of the soft French spring, many varieties of roses were in bud. I am sure that many a French princess has walked the paths of this garden. Today, a small terrace with gay umbrellas invited 20th-century guests to enjoy the blue skies, warm sun, and gentle breezes.

A few hours earlier, approaching the entrance, I realized for the first time that a chateau is really a castle. As in all of the chateaux hotels I visited, the walls were formidable and high, with towers at some of the corners. The walls were rough and forbidding and the doors quite narrow. Once inside, the interior is a marked contrast to the rude exterior.

There are six lodging rooms in le Besset, all of them carefully

furnished in different French periods. It is indeed a French castle hotel of the first class. Great attention has been given to making every room as authentic as possible. Each has a marvelous view of the countryside.

By way of interesting changes, the Tower Room is furnished in the period of the 1930s. It has a bed with a beautiful suede bedspread, modern lighting fixtures, and tables with glass tops. This chrome and glass did seem a little strange with all the Louis XII and Louis XIV decor in the remainder of the castle.

I asked some other guests about the food. They replied that although off the beaten track, le Besset had the reputation for being one of the finest restaurants in France. Menu specialties included rabbit, lobster, salad, fresh salmon, and filet of sole. One lady was rather intrigued with the idea that ladies have their own menus without prices.

The Chateau du Besset is an intimate, luxurious experience and deserves more than merely a single night. Active sports—horseback riding, tennis, and swimming are available. The walks in the park and drives around the countryside provide the opportunity to contemplate life in its quiet, graceful, harmonious moods.

LE CHATEAU DU BESSET (Relais et Chateaux), 07130 St.-Romain-de-Lerps (near Saint Peray). Tel.: (75) 44-41-63. A 6-guestroom exceptionally comfortable 15th-century castle with first-class service in the beautiful Burgundy countryside, 15 km. from Valence. Breakfast, lunch, dinner. Beautiful parkland walks, horseback riding, swimming pool, tennis courts on grounds. Closed Oct. 2 to Apr. 27. Rates: See Index.

Directions: Michelin sect. map 93. Follow N-86 south and turn right on D-533 at the town of St. Peray. Watch for the signs for St.-Romain-de-Lerps and after driving about 10 km. to that village, turn left and follow signs back into the country about 5 km. Coming north or south on the Autoroute A-7 (sometimes called Autoroute du Soleil) exit at Valence, and cross the Rhone River Bridge to St. Peray.

HOSTELLERIE LA CARDINALE, Baix (Ardèche)

I was now back for the second time in the riverside village of Baix and would be revisiting one of the places that I had seen on my first trip to France a few years ago. I was anxious to meet the relatively new owners, with whom I had been in correspondence. Route N-86 became the village street and sure enough there was a signpost pointing to the left toward the river, indicating that La Cardinale was a short but welcome distance from the main road.

As with a few other accommodations in this book, the Hostellerie La Cardinale is a member of the Relais et Chateaux group, but is distinguished by the fact that its original proprietor, M. Tillot, conceived the idea of forming Relais et Chateaux, an organization of small hotels of culinary distinction, with the purpose of promoting one another.

Of course, the building had not changed; it probably hasn't changed since August of 1642, when Cardinal Richelieu apparently remained here overnight on a journey from Paris. On the day of my visit the very attractive terrace with colorful umbrellas had a few other Sunday patrons, and the flowers of late May were in interesting contrast to the texture of the ancient brickwork.

The new proprietors are all members of the Motte family, and fortunately they speak excellent conversational English. They were kind enough to invite me for lunch on the terrace and I must admit that I was charmed by the attractive mother and daughter, as well as by the pleasant fish served in a light wine sauce with tiny onions and a side dish of rice. My notes indicate the mashed potatoes were so light and fluffy they must have been run through the blender more than once.

I was extremely curious to know whether or not they had received many guests as a result of being included in the earlier edition of this book, and they were delighted to draw my attention to their guest register, where many Americans had mentioned *CIBR, Europe* in their comments. Incidentally, nothing pleases me quite so much as receiving letters from travelers who have stayed at places I have recommended. I feel as if we all belong to a very special little club, and I love to receive notes about your adventures.

La Cardinale is not as grand as some of the other Relais members, but quality and taste are certainly evident in the sitting and dining rooms and guest rooms. All have been furnished in beautiful French antiques, as well as with several contemporary paintings, and the atmosphere is easy and comfortable.

Just a few minutes away there are other guest rooms and sitting rooms in another building, La Résidence, located on a height of land with a broader view of the river and a definite feeling of luxury in the country.

HOSTELLERIE LA CARDINALE (Relais et Chateaux), 07210 Baix. Tel.: (75) 62-85-88. A 15-guestroom village inn overlooking the Rhone River, approx. 130 km. south of Lyon. Besides lodgings in the main inn, there are rooms in La Residence on a hillside outside the village. Breakfast, lunch, & dinner. Private swimming pool. Tennis and horseback riding nearby. Closed Oct. 1 to Mar. 1. Rates: See Index.

Directions: Baix is on N-86 south of Le Pouzin. If on A-7 or N-6, you can cross the river at Le Pouzin or Montelinar. Baix is actually part of Rochenaure.

LE PRIEURÉ, Villeneuve-les-Avignon

Avignon is one of the showplaces of southeastern France. It is rich in history, tradition, scenery. The countryside is dotted with names that are rich in meaning—Arles, where Van Gogh painted some of his sunlit landscapes; Aix-en-Provence, the capital that has been a great artistic center for centuries; Grenoble, surrounded by clifflike mountains; Marseille, filled with art museums and ancient monuments; and Avignon, itself the seat of the Papacy in the 14th century, dominated by the Pope's palace, a fortress sometimes austere and sometimes luxurious, complete with watchtowers and frescoes.

Such historic and artistic wealth makes Le Prieuré, located as it is at the double gateway to both Spain and the Riviera, one of the most sought-after accommodations in the south of France.

Located in Villeneuve-les-Avignon, a small town across the Rhone River from the much larger city of Avignon, it is much more quiet and less tourist-oriented than its larger neighbor.

With guests from all parts of the world gathered on the terrace and beside the swimming pool, Le Prieuré's atmosphere is decidedly cosmopolitan. Conversations flow in German, English, French, and Japanese, with everyone quite willing to share their travel adventures.

For hundreds of years the inn was a priory; more recently it has become a hotel of the first class presided over by a most pleasant, urban innkeeper, Jacques Mille, who, like a good many innkeepers, has learned to be affable in any language.

The hotel and gardens reminded me very much of the gardens in the Alhambra in Granada, with their carefully tended irises and roses, small evergreen hedges, and conical-shaped evergreens that

seem to grow everywhere in the Mediterranean countries. In the morning, the bees were buzzing among the ivy in the breathtakingly bright sunshine of Provence. The walk to the parking area is through a long, arched rose trellis.

Guest rooms for the most part are contemporary in design, and my room, with its one glass wall and sliding door leading out to a balcony that overlooked the swimming pool and tennis courts, had bright modern furniture and draperies. Meals are served in the gardens under the trees.

I made a return visit to see Jacques Mille, who is the most

Americanized Frenchman I have ever met. It was a wonderful pleasure to sit in the new dining room with him and listen to his bubbling enthusiasm about the changes that have been made. "The chimney and fireplace were moved, stone by stone, and replaced here in the new part," he pointed out. Several new bedrooms have also been added.

"Of course, our guests still continue to use this as a touring base for visiting Avignon, and we have our own group of ancient buildings, called La Chartreuse, which at one time was an abbey."

HOSTELLERIE LE PRIEURÉ (Relais et Chateaux), 7 Place du Chapitre, Villeneuve-les-Avignon, 30400 Avignon. Tel.: (90) 25-18-20. A 38-guestroom very comfortable inn in the center of one of France's most popular historic and cultural regions. Breakfast, lunch, and dinner. Swimming pool, two tennis courts on grounds. Within a very short distance of the town of Avignon. Closed Nov. 1 to Mar. 1. Rates: See Index.

Directions: Michelin sect. map 81, 93. From the north via the Autoroute: note that at Orange, about 10 km. north of Avignon, A-7, the main autoroute from Paris to Nice, is a junction for A-9 which goes to northern Spain. Use the Avignon exit on either of these two autoroutes and Villeneuve is on the west side of the Rhone River. If using N-86 from the north, turn east at Bagnols and follow N-580 into Villeneuve.

L'AUBERGE DE NOVES, Noves

Monsieur Lalleman, enjoying a respite from his duties as host of this delightful inn just south of Avignon, joined me on the terrace where I was having lunch.

When I remarked about the leisurely service, he responded, "Here at Auberge de Noves there is no hurrying the meal. Even our salads are made especially. They are not waiting in the refrigerator to be served. All of this takes time."

In the meantime, I noticed him keeping a watchful eye on the waiter who was making this selfsame salad of fresh watercress, chopped shallots, and greens all mixed in a handsome silver bowl. Carrots, mushrooms, onions, lettuce, and sliced tomatoes were added. When I remarked that the salad would seem to be a meal in itself, he shrugged and said, "This is only a side dish."

It was a beautiful day in the south of France. The birds in the garden were everywhere, chirping, singing, whistling, and fighting. The flowers were already in full bloom. Butterflies were flitting from table to table, and guests, having completed their meal, were going for leisurely walks through the quite extensive gardens.

The arrival of some freshly made sliced paté launched M. Lalleman into a short dissertation. "We have many kinds of paté," he said. "In fact, the chef in any good French restaurant is able to make his own particular creation. Ours does wonders with rabbit, duck, and goose liver, but a good paté can be made from many combinations

of ingredients." He excused himself for just a moment, while I watched the waiter at the next table deftly carve and debone two delicious-looking roast ducklings. Seeing my interest, the guests at the table offered me a succulent morsel. It was delicious.

Following lunch, my host showed me through many of the guest rooms of the inn, all gaily decorated, and he pointed with pride to the swimming pool in the garden which, during less clement days, has a plastic bubble placed over it. There was a view across the meadow to ancient towers in the distance.

L'AUBERGE DE NOVES (Relais et Chateaux), 13550 Noves. Tel.: (90) 94-19-21. A 22-guestroom very comfortable Provence manor house a few km. south of Avignon. Breakfast, lunch, and dinner. Swimming pool on grounds. Tennis and fishing nearby. Closed Jan. to mid-Feb. Rates: See Index.

Directions: Michelin sect. maps 81, 93. Autoroute A-7 use the Avignon Sud exit. Follow N-7 across the river, take first right and the next main right. Go about 1 km. and look for sign on left.

DOMAINE DE CHATEAUNEUF, Nans-les-Pins

A traveler from Paris to Nice or Cannes on the autoroutes would do well to stop his headlong flight and remain here for a few days just to let the serenity and tranquility of southern France envelop him.

The Chateauneuf is in a center of thickly wooded parkland, surrounded by 250 acres of vineyards and forests. On the day of my visit, the chestnut trees were in bloom, the birds were singing, and there were white doves restlessly circling the chateau. The courtyard was flooded with sunlight filtering through the leaves and a warm, spring breeze gently wafted its way among the flowers. I could have remained a week.

As my hostess explained, this is an 18th-century chateau that has seen the passing of royalty in France, the horrors of the Terror, and the glories of the Empire. "It is still here now," she said, "as peaceful and as calm as ever."

"Elegant but informal" are the words that occur to me. The lodgings are all very pleasant, with comfortable chateau furniture and many oils and water colors. The dining room overlooks the park, and in warm weather meals are taken outside.

Of particular interest to me was a corner room on the main floor with a collection of local crafts: scarves, handkerchiefs, dolls, jewelry, and similar items all presented in a most attractive way.

The two tennis courts were in use while I was there, and the pool had some midday swimmers. My hostess told me that, unlike St. Tropez, eighty kilometers to the east, there are separate sunning areas for both ladies and gentlemen in this chateau.

The Domaine de Chateauneuf indeed is quiet and tranquil. It is the south of France the way I hoped to find it.

DOMAINE DE CHATEAUNEUF (Relais et Chateaux), 83860 Nans-les-Pins. Tel.: (94) 78-90-06. A 29-guestroom comfortable but simple 18th-century manor house with its own beautiful park, 150 km. west of Cannes and 45 km. east of Marseille. Breakfast, lunch, and dinner. Swimming pool and tennis courts on grounds. Horseback riding,

golf, fishing, and other recreation nearby. Closed Nov. 3 to Apr. 30.
Rates: See Index.

Directions: Michelin sect. map 84. Exit Autoroute A-8 at St. Maximin.
Follow N-560 south and watch for D-80, which leads to village of
Nans-les-Pins.

LA BASTIDE DE TOURTOUR, Salernes

For postal purposes this castle-hotel is located in Salernes, one
of the villages near the larger city of Draguignan. As far as I am
concerned, it is located in the extremely scenic village of Tourtour,
which, I learned, is pronounced "too-too" (the "r" being silent).

La Bastide de Tourtour is situated in one of the most picturesque
and attractive landscapes in Provence—on a promontory almost
2,000 feet above sea level with a very impressive view of the countryside. The inn is set in the middle of a great pine forest.

While sitting at the pool I learned just how convenient it is to all
the scenic attractions in this section of Provence. I struck up an

acquaintance with a couple from Atlanta, Georgia, who came for two days and were now extending their stay for a week. "I can't imagine a better place to enjoy the south of France," was one of the most frequently repeated phrases. "It's only about an hour and a half to Cannes, Nice, and St. Tropez, and we took a day trip to the Verdon Gorges and went over to Monte Carlo. We stopped and had lunch at the Chevre d'Or. I hope you will go there." (I did.)

This inn is in a most imposing restored castle, whose austere beige-colored walls and towers of native stone belie the luxurious interiors. The heavy stone arches and beamed ceilings in the reception hall and living and dining rooms have all been gracefully accented with golden upholstery and draperies. It is a memorable scene, particularly in the evening when candles are lit on every table.

It is obvious that the owners and innkeepers have taken a personal pride in the lodging rooms, all of which are furnished most luxuriously. Many of them have their own balconies with a panoramic view that stretches for over 100 kilometers.

My friends from Georgia were most enthusiastic about the food, emphasizing the fact that they had already had three dinners, each with a different specialty. "We like to drive around in the daytime and get a lunch of bread and cheese," they said, "but it is such a joy to return here in the late afternoon, go for a swim, and then rest until dinnertime. I hope you won't tell too many people about it."

LA BASTIDE DE TOURTOUR (Relais et Chateaux), 83690 Tourtour. Tel.: (94) 70-57-30. A 26-guestroom very comfortable restored castle in the high hills of Var (Provence), 100 km. from Nice. Breakfast, lunch, and dinner. Swimming pool and tennis courts on grounds. Beautiful walks, back roads, and gorgeous views nearby. Closed Oct. 3 to April 28. Rates: See Index.

Directions: Michelin sect. map 84. Draguignan follow D-49 (spectacular road) to Ampus. Turn left on the road to St. Pierre de Tourtour and Tourtour. Alternate road is D-557 out of Draguignan to a point outside of Villecroze. Turn right on D-51 to Tourtour.

The Marketplace at Draguignan

It was ten o'clock in the morning and the entire plaza at Draguignan was now the weekly farmers' market. Earlier in the day, the farm trucks had chugged into the square with loads of carrots, cauliflowers, potatoes, beans, enormous green peppers, artichokes, bananas, oranges, strawberries, eggplants, pineapples, and dozens of fresh fruits and vegetables. Stalls and tables appeared almost miraculously, offering cheeses in every flavor and style, poultry, meats, fish, flowers, pastries, and even pet hamsters and rabbits.

It was a gorgeous, sunny day and to protect the tables, canopies and umbrellas were quickly put up. Some musicians were holding forth in one corner.

I bought a sweet roll in the bakery and some milk in the butcher shop and sat down on the bench to enjoy the scene. A little French girl in a beautiful blue dress that matched her eyes, came and sat down next to me and solemnly offered me a bite of her delicious chocolate ice cream cone. It was too much to resist, chocolate has always been my favorite.

CHATEAU DE TRIGANCE, Trigance

It distresses me to realize that a great many people are going to visit Provence, the Cote d'Azur, and the Riviera and not find their way to these magnificent mountains and the truly breathtaking beauty of the Verdon Gorges. A day-trip from Cannes or Nice would be enhanced by a stop at Trigance for lunch.

Not that Chateau de Trigance is undiscovered. Far from it. In looking at the guest list I found that a great many well-known people from all over the world had apparently studied the road maps and found their way to this wild, wonderful country and its 11th-century fortress-castle.

First of all, there is the walk up the steps. The castle was built on the top of the hill to prevent besiegers from reaching it, and there is no way of avoiding the climb. However, once reaching the battlements at the top, the feeling of exhilaration is so great that the ascent is soon forgotten. Here I was, surrounded by a ring of mountains and I could just imagine what dramas had been enacted on this site for a thousand years.

There are only eight guest rooms in this fortress; however, all of the conveniences have been added and everything is very comfortable. The main dining room is carved out of the rock, and the atmosphere is definitely medieval.

While meandering around the castle, I came upon something that still raises the hair on the back of my head. I walked through the dining room and down some stone steps into a very dark and some-

what gloomy tower. Seeing the sunlight filtering through a narrow window, I stepped into a room, and there in front of me was a woman with grey hair dressed in medieval costume. A very fierce-looking man was standing next to her. They looked so real I was frightened. Then I laughed as I realized they were only papier mâché figures.

Two of my closest neighbors, Ruth and George Ripley, made a stop at Chateau Trigance a few years ago. "Absolutely spectacular," is the way Ruth Ripley describes it.

CHATEAU DE TRIGANCE (Relais et Chateau), 83840 Trigance. Tel.: (94) 76-91-18. An 8-guestroom comfortable but simple inn located in an ancient 11th-century castle near the entrance to the Verdon Gorges. Breakfast, lunch, and dinner. Closed Nov. to Easter. Rates: See Index.

Directions: This will take some persistence, but it is well worth it. Locate Draguignan on Michelin map #84. Follow D-955 north through Montferrat, through the military reservation, north to Riblaquon. Trigance is about 4 km. to the northeast on D-90. This is about 10 km. from the Verdon Gorges. Leaving the car in the parking space, carry a minimum amount of luggage and walk the 175 steps up the side of the precipice and along the path to the reception desk.

Les Gorges du Verdon

As incredible as it seemed, just a few hours earlier I had been sunning myself on a Riviera beach under a blue Mediterranean sky. Now, I was standing on the rim of a high cliff, looking down into the depth of the Verdon Gorges in the northern part of Provence. This is an area of absolutely breathtaking views, with bridges soaring over the deep chasms, and villages so precariously perched on the top of rocky precipices that they seem almost ready to topple over into oblivion.

This is a place where even the widest-angle lens does not capture the view. The road leads through several tunnels plunging down next to the river and then twisting up treacherously, clinging to the sides of the cliff to the very top of the rim. It reminded me of the volcanic crater on the island of La Palma in the Canary Islands.

HOTEL LE CAGNARD, Cagnes

Talk to anyone who has been to Le Cagnard and invariably they will roll their eyes to heaven and say "Unbelievable." Looking back on it I am not sure that it ever happened. Le Cagnard is part of a medieval fortress called Haut de Cagnes, overlooking the city of Cagnes and a considerable expanse of the Mediterranean. Viewed from a distance, the permutations of towers, bridges, walls, and crenelated battlements exist in a bluish, purplish haze. The amazing thing is that inside this walled promontory are churches, nightclubs, restaurants, art galleries, jazz clubs, hundred of apartments, an outdoor park, narrow streets in which it is very easy to get lost, hundreds of steps (all of which seem to go up), and a definite shortage of parking spaces.

The hotel is perched precariously, but safely, on the outer walls. My room was on the very top of one of the towers, and its somewhat monastic air was relieved by a white ceiling, blue walls, reproductions of Van Gogh, and red furniture with blue flowers. My casement windows had a glorious view looking down into the town and out across the sea. I sat cross-legged in this window, watching early-morning Cagnes come to life.

The dining room looks as if it has been carved right out of granite, with a vaulted ceiling and a small balcony; when the long Riviera twilight descends and the candles are lit, it is indeed very romantic. The specialties on the menu are *carre d'Agneaux aux herbes de Provence*, and *Daurade flambée au pastis*. They also serve an impressive bouillabaisse.

Off the dining room there is an absolutely glorious little balcony decorated with geraniums, which I shared with several other guests who fell into two categories—people who were visiting for the first time, whose conversation was based on their adventures in locating Le Cagnard, and those blasé many-timers who by now knew their

way around and had their favorite little shops and small streets. It is very popular with Americans. We all agreed that if you liked it, you liked it a lot.

HOTEL LE CAGNARD (Relais et Chateaux), 06800 Cagnes-sur-Mer. Tel.: (93) 20-73-21. A 14-guestroom comfortable but simple inn located in a castle high above the town of Cagnes-sur-Mer in the Alpes-Maritimes. It is situated about midway between Cannes and Nice. Breakfast, lunch, and dinner served daily. Within a short drive of the Riviera beaches. Closed from Nov. 1 to mid-Dec. Rates: See Index.

Directions: Michelin sect. map 84. From Autoroute A-8 (the main road to Cannes and Nice) use Cagnes Sortie (exit). Bear to the right at sign for Cagnes-Vence. Do not take the first left that goes up the hill, nor the road to left marked Grasse, but continue on to a roundabout (traffic circle) and follow the road to Vence. This leads through the town of Cagnes. The key words are "Haut de Cagnes." Start looking for this sign on the right when the road to Vence leads up a hill. Turn right and follow a twisting road to the top. There are a few signs for the hotel. Take road as far as you can and walk the rest of the way to the reception. I had a comically exasperating time locating this place.

LE CHATEAU DU DOMAINE ST.-MARTIN, Vence

It was a beautiful warm day on the French Riviera. I had taken the road from Cagnes to Vence and following the signs to Coursegoules, could see the Chateau St.-Martin high in the hills above me. It looked most impressive. The road wound upward and I found myself at the entrance, which was the well-restored ruins of an ancient drawbridge, now permanently open.

Even before the construction of the original castle and drawbridge by the Knights Templars after their return from the Crusades in

the 12th century, St.-Martin already had a history, since it was named for a Bishop of Tours and an evangelist to the Gauls who had lived here as early as A.D. 350.

I walked through the courtyard and through the doors leading into the entryway. Inside, I found an elegant, formal atmosphere with many tapestries, arched windows, rich-looking furniture, and many oils and prints. There were several guests enjoying luncheon in the dining room and on the balcony, which had an awesome view from its 1,500-foot elevation.

When Harry Truman visited many years ago, he told the owners that they really needed a swimming pool, so they built one and called it the Truman Swimming Pool. There are tennis courts on the estate and the golf course is not far away.

In the main building of the Chateau St.-Martin are seventeen *très élégantes* bedrooms, most of them reached by climbing the richly carved marble staircase to the second floor. Many of them have views of the town, countryside, and the Mediterranean from their balconies. There are additional guest rooms in small, individual Provençal country houses on the estate.

The atmosphere was extraordinarily light, peaceful, and quiet. Fresh summer nights and sunny days make it ideal for a tranquil vacation experience. It is just fifteen minutes from the Mediterranean, and within a short drive of the old medieval town of Vence, with its art gallery with works by Dufy, Carzou, and Chagall. The Matisse Chapel in Vence is world-famous.

In reading the brochure about the Chateau St.-Martin (which incidentally has a four-star luxury category), as nearly as I am able to understand, all of the rates include both breakfast and dinner with no exceptions. It might be well to double-check this when making reservations.

LE CHATEAU DU DOMAINE ST.-MARTIN (Relais et Chateaux), 06140 Vence. Tel.: (93) 58-02-02. A 28-guestroom exceptionally comfortable hotel with first-class service on the heights overlooking Vence and the Riviera in the Alpes-Maritimes; 30 km. from Cannes, and 16 km. from Nice. Breakfast, lunch, dinner. Swimming pool and tennis courts on grounds. Golf nearby. Short distance from Matisse Chapel in Vence. Closed Dec., Jan., and Feb. Rates: See Index.

Directions: Michelin section map 84. Follow the road D-36 from Cagnes to Vence. In Vence look for signs for Coursegoules and then Chateau St.-Martin.

CHATEAU DE LA CHEVRE D'OR, Eze Village

"This may be the most beautiful view on the Cote d'Azur." It was twilight. Three of us were seated on the patio of Chevre d'Or, overlooking the Mediterranean, quietly absorbing the delicate shadings of color as daylight turned to darkness. These sentiments were expressed by Judy, who with her husband Alvin, had been traveling up the Italian Riviera into France, visiting several attractive hotels en route. "Perhaps it is the night, the company, and our beautiful day all coming together, but I have never seen anything like this before and probably never will again." We all nodded in silent agreement.

Chevre d'Or is at the top of the highest point of Eze Village, which can be seen from some distance away traveling up the Moyenne Corniche. It is, according to the *Michelin Green Guide* for the French Riviera, "A prime example of a perched village clinging like an eagle's nest to a rock spike towering 1,550 feet overlooking the sea." Caution. There are two communities named Eze. One is Eze Mer, on the edge of the Mediterranean Sea, and the other is Eze Village, some distance above. Artists and craftsmen had set up stalls and shops in the village, and I purchased a very handsome watercolor of Eze, which is reproduced on the cover of this editon.

The innkeeper is Monsieur Bruno Ingold, a sophisticated, cordial Swiss gentleman. His staff is headed by the headwaiter, Claude, who works deftly from table to table, preparing the many French specialties, overseeing the service, and conversing expertly in many different languages.

The few guest rooms are in a romantic style and, incredible as it may seem, innkeeper Ingold has created a very small swimming pool on the tiny terrace. It is most welcome for a quick plunge during the sunny season.

La Chevre d'Or is always booked considerably in advance for July and August, but between the 20th of August and the 10th of October it might be possible to call the day before and reserve a room. This is an excellent time to be on the Riviera, the sun is still high, the water is still warm, and most important, the crowds are far thinner.

While we were talking, night had fallen completely and the deep blackness was punctuated by the pearl-like pinpoints of moving lights as cars traversed the roadway below. It is all really much beyond my meager powers of description.

CHATEAU DE LA CHEVRE D'OR (Relais et Chateaux), 06360 Eze Village. Tel.: (93) 41-12-12. A 9-guestroom very comfortable inn clinging by its fingernails to the cliffs high over the Mediterranean, about 12 km. from Nice. Breakfast, lunch, and dinner. Small swimming pool on grounds. Tennis nearby. This is an excellent place to stay (as are all of the others in this section of France) to enjoy the recreation on the Riviera. Closed Nov. to Mar. Rates: See Index.

Directions: Michelin sect. map 84. Eze Village is located on the Moyenne (Middle) Corniche (N-7). After reaching Eze Village turn right at the first road after the bus park at a sign that says, "Tourist Information." Follow this road to the parking area for the village. Lock your car, don't take your bags, walk up the ancient stone steps through an alley to a sign with a goat's head on it. Bear left through a narrow ancient street that winds around the outside and persist until you reach the front door of the inn. They will send someone back for your bags and tell you how to solve the parking problem.

Itinerary Number Two—Dover, Calais, Normandy, the Marne, the Wine Road, Savoie, Avignon-Montfavet, les Baux, Arles, Marseille.

Most of the reservations on this itinerary were made on a day-by-day basis. There is some overlap with Itinerary Number One; however, it is not significant.

HOTEL WINDSOR, Calais

For many visitors to France who do not go directly to Paris, Calais is one of the principal ports of entry, the others being Boulogne, Dieppe, and Le Havre.

Leaving France, Calais is an open gateway to England, thanks to the large number of ships and hovercraft routes. It is an excursion

center for travel to Kent and the towns and seaside resorts of Folke-
stone, Dover, Deal, Sandwich, Ramsgate, Margate, and Canterbury.

After taking the train from Victoria Station to Dover, I experienced some delays because of labor problems and eventually took a
hovercraft across the channel, an interesting adventure lasting only
thirty minutes.

I picked up my AutoEurope car and after making a decision to
stay in Calais for one night before continuing, I decided to do what
many other Americans and Britons have done—I asked the advice of
the attendant in the auto rental office about a medium-priced hotel
in the town. It's interesting how decisions that seem rather small at
first can play such an important role in certain aspects of a traveler's
adventures.

The Hotel Windsor was a very pleasant, medium-priced hotel
about fifteen minutes by car from the port of entry. Let me further say
that the particular area in which it is located seemed to be highly
tourist-oriented and there are several restaurants and other hotels as
well. However, I discovered the next morning as I was leaving Calais
that there is a whole second city that presents quite a different aspect.
Had the car rental man suggested a hotel in the larger, less tourist-
oriented area I would have had an entirely different experience. The
line between these two sections is bounded by an impressive Rodin
sculpture of the six Calais burghers who offered to sacrifice their lives
in exchange for the lifting of the seige against the city at that time.

The Windsor is typical of other medium-priced hotels in the
same class. The price included a *douche*, the French word for shower
bath. The toilet facilities are down the hall. The room was very
comfortable, quite large, had two beds, and the shower and
washbowl were in a separate little room. There was one lamp over
each bed and one central overhead lamp, no other lamps on the
tables. It was clean, and the wallpaper was very pleasant. The cost
included *petit déjeuner* (breakfast), which consisted of French bread,
a croissant or two, some jellies and jams, and either hot coffee or hot
chocolate. These are served in a small separate room, which seemed
to be the custom throughout the country. There were no restaurant
facilities at the hotel.

French, English, and Italian were spoken, and the innkeeper
was very agreeable.

My stay at the Windsor gives rise to the advice that it is a good
idea to take a room on what might be called the "quiet side" of a
hotel, and to make sure there are no neon lights shining in the

window after dark. When choosing a hotel in a town or a small city, try to avoid one located on a main thoroughfare.

HOTEL WINDSOR, 2 Rue du Commandant Bonningue, 62100 Calais. Tel.: (21) 34-59-40. A typical, medium-sized hotel in the more tourist-oriented section of Calais, about 15 min. from port of entry. Clean, comfortable rooms with wc down the hall. Continental breakfast included in price of room. English is spoken. Open all year. Rates: See Index.

Directions: Calais, like other French ports, has ferry and/or hovercraft connections with England. Get a good map of northern France (Michelin 998 will be very nicely, also Michelin 51).

LE VERT MESNIL, Tilques

I departed Calais in the rain but with high hopes, and driving along the N-43 I saw a sign for this chateau and decided to take a look. I was to do this several times on this trip to France with varying results.

This time, however, it proved to be a fortuitous move because the chateau was set back in a quiet park and had many very attractive features, including some gardens, tennis courts, and pleasant walks in the forest.

I was greeted in French by a somewhat austere concierge who put me in charge of a young chambermaid wearing red toenail polish and open-toed sandals. The two of us continued on a tour of many of the bedrooms, most of which had high ceilings and very pleasing views of the lawns and park. Some of the rooms had been decorated

recently to include wc's, and some of the bathrooms were particularly impressive.

The restaurant had a marble floor and rather formal covered chairs and an intimate view of a stable courtyard on one side and beautiful front gardens and lawn on the other. The prices and menu appeared to be a good value.

This would be an excellent stop for a traveler arriving in or departing from Calais. It is only about forty kilometers from the port and, I think, creates a very pleasant lasting impression of French hospitality. There was little English spoken here, but lots of understanding of English, if you get my drift.

LE VERT MESNIL, Tilques, 62500 St.-Omer. Tel.: (21) 93-28-99. A 40-guestroom chateau-hotel with restaurant, 40 km. from Calais, in a park setting. All of the rooms have private bathrooms and telephones. Tennis, volleyball, gardens, and forest walks. Very little English spoken. Rates: See Index.

Directions: Tilques is a small village on the N-43 between Ardres and St.-Omer. Michelin 51 shows greater detail.

HOSTELLERIE LE RELAIS, Bayenghem par Lumbres

This is the last of three accommodations that are accessible from Calais. Located just a few miles from Saint-Omer toward Boulogne, it would also be a good overnight stop out of the former town as well.

I had tried to phone this place from the auto-rental office in Calais without success. (If you don't speak French, don't try to telephone small country places in France.) It is in a little town off the N-42, but is well signposted to the left in the village. In a rather old building with some impressive gardens and a sunny terrace, it is run by madame with a little help from monsieur; I don't believe I got their names, but it is not important.

What is important is that it has a very quiet, hospitable atmosphere and is about as unspoiled as one could find. There are three pleasant, although somewhat austere, rooms overlooking the gardens and the farm area and one of them has a nice brass double bed with a comforter and washbowl in the room. It could be a very agreeable place to stay—not commercial like the Windsor in Calais or "resorty" like the chateau at the last stop. I think "French natural" would be a good description.

The day of my visit they were having a special luncheon to

celebrate a confirmation, and the dining room looked particularly attractive. Madame does all of the cooking and if it is typical of other similar accommodations that I visited, I'm sure it's excellent.

HOSTELLERIE LE RELAIS, Bayenghem par Lumbres 62380. Tel.: (21) 39-64-54. A 3-guestroom, hospitable inn with a pleasant dining room in a small, quiet village, a few miles from St.-Omer. No English is spoken. Rates: See Index.

Directions: Lumbres is on N-42 between Boulogne and St.-Omer. Michelin 51

Normandy

This is the country of cream, cider, and calvados. One of the ways to see it is to stay at private chateaux. The idea is not new to France, but the spirit in which Bertrand Laffilé organized his association is new. One must be an accepted member of his club, the Demeures Club, in order to be welcomed as a guest in the thirty-five chateaux in his organization, most of which are in western France. There is a membership fee of 800 francs per family, but it is well worth it if one plans to visit more than two places, because the prices of rooms are very low (150 to 300 francs) compared to other more commercial accommodations.

In each chateau, there are no more than two guest rooms, and the chatelains have pledged to receive no more than one party at a time, therefore providing a really personal welcome for their guests. It is an interesting arrangement because the chateau owners enjoy the opportunity to meet new people, and they are usually people who are in love with their chateau, who have made some sacrifice to keep it going. Conversely, guests have the opportunity to experience life in a French home and to enjoy these very beautiful chateaux at a most reasonable price

For further information, write to Bertrand Laffilé, Demeures Club, 5 Place du Marché Sainte Catherine, 75004 Paris, France.

PARFONDEVAL, Londinières

No one seemed to stir as I rang the doorbell repeatedly. I peered through the windows, then pushed the door open, and called softly, then louder...still only silence. Boldly I entered the vaulted hall, perceived a stairway, went up, discovered a most exquisite little

antique boudoir, its walls adorned with panels of chinoiserie, that opened onto a sloping lawn. Suddenly, two small children burst in with a roar, followed by an elegant lady farmer, Jennifer Armand-De-lille, our hostess.

"Have a cup of tea," she said. I sat down with her and one of her friends from New York, who had come to spend a few days. We soon found common ground and enjoyed a chat that lasted until it was time to think of dinner.

After going to Harvard and starting life as a banker, Frederic Armand-Delille decided to follow in his father's footsteps and raise cattle on his mother's property, Parfondeval. At the time, she was still living there with her husband, art historian Kenneth Clark. She has now left the house and all its furnishings to Frederic and Jennifer. It is a marvelous stately and quiet home, with nothing commerical about it. A guest really feels like a member of the family, something like a distant cousin, and the house itself is welcoming. My room was full of antiques and had a lovely, quaint bathroom, well provided with scented soaps and other miscellaneous amenities. After breakfast, the next morning, I helped Jennifer feed the lambs before going off towards the sea and a marvelous lunch at Les Quatre Pains.

PARFONDEVAL, Saint Pierre des Jonquiéres, 76660 Londinières. Tel.: (35) 93-85-22 (at meal times). A 2-guestroom (private baths) small chateau. Breakfast and/or dinner may be arranged with Jen-

nifer. Open year-round except Christmas and from mid-July to mid-Aug. Rates: See Index.

Directions: Take D-915 from Paris to Forges les Eaux, then take D-1314 to Neufchâtel and Londinières. Continue towards Smermesnil for 2 km. Parfondeval is at the end of a long private drive.

LES QUATRE PAINS RESTAURANT, Tocqueville sur Eu

One doesn't believe it when one gets there. The place looks a bit too new and untrustworthy. But the welcome is friendly and the menu appetizing. I orderd a mussel soup that was really delicious and very reasonable. I noticed some wonderful-looking dishes that other diners were eating with great gusto. The desserts looked scrumptious, and I had a marvelously light and strongly flavored tarte aux fraises. People go to restaurants for all sorts of silly reasons, but this is one to visit just for good food. The average price per person is about 150 francs, including wine.

LES QUATRE PAINS RESTAURANT, Tocqueville sur Eu, 76910 Criel sur Mer. Tel.: (35) 86-75-40. A perfect bistro on the way to the sea from Parfondeval. J. and G. Brachais, Owners.

Directions: On the seaside road, D-925, between Le Tréport and Dieppe.

LE MOULIN DE FOURGES, Ecos

Sleeping Beauty's house. I felt I was having a very convincing dream. Turning off the main road into a smaller road, I went through a little village, taking a narrower road into a thick forest of beautiful tall oaks and chestnuts that suddenly opened up to reveal a river, the Epte. On the river was the most perfect millhouse anyone could imagine. The location was green and quiet, the building was right out of a storybook, complete with a large waterwheel, mossy roof, and welcoming cat. When I arrived it was raining, but everything was bright and shiny inside.

Lunch is served in a narrow dining room with windows on the water, looking out beyond the forest. You can try all the typical dishes of Normandy, including a fish soup made with cider, tripe, and anything made from or with apples, the Norman fruit. Don't forget to ask for a "trou normand," a little glass of calvados (liquor of apples), in between the different dishes.

This, in all respects, is a typical French place, for its qualities and its shortcomings. The service, especially on weekends, is a little slow, and the downstairs bathrooms are not the brightest I have seen. But the rooms are nice and the whole place is so amazingly pleasant and simple that I think it's worth it.

LE MOULIN DE FOURGES, Fourges, 27630 Ecos. Tel.: (32) 52-12-12. A simple, picturesque millhouse inn with a good restaurant, some rooms with showers. Closed Mon. and Tues. Rates: See Index.

Directions: Take the Autoroute de l'Ouest from Paris; exit Mantes Est towards Vetheuil, La Roche Guyon, and then north to Amenucourt (pretty view of the Seine Valley). Take road D-37 from there.

HOTEL BELLE VUE, Coucy-le-Château (Aisne)

I was enjoying a post-dinner constitutional around the small village of Coucy-le-Château, which sits on a height of land and has great fortifications on all four sides. I passed through a triangular-shaped village square and noted quite a few buildings of Dutch design. I understand that Flemish architectural influence is quite extensive in this part of France. It's really not very far from the Belgium border.

The day had started in Calais, and in midafternoon, after visiting a few accommodations, I decided to telephone ahead to the Hotel Belle Vue to make a room reservation for the evening. I soon discovered that no English was spoken here and after resorting to a few halting French idioms (I'd suggest you have such phrases and others available at all times), I was sufficiently assured in French that I would be welcome.

I'm going to elaborate a bit because as I subsequently discovered this was a typical middle-range accommodation and I found many of the same features and drawbacks in other similar places.

For one thing, this was my first overnight visit in a place where not even a modicum of English was spoken. I was glad to have a simple phrase book, including some translations of French menu items. Later on, I didn't need it, but at the start of the trip I had to become adjusted once again.

First, the bedrooms. They were pleasant and comfortable, al-

though two people would have found my room with two beds rather cramped. There was only one light in the room and that was between the two beds. The bedroom had a washbowl and a bidet. There was pleasant blue wallpaper and the beds were reasonably comfortable, although there was a certain austere quality in that not all of the beds had cotton sheets.

The greatest emphasis here was on the dining room and I later learned that the evening meal was typical of many I would have—reasonably priced and delicious. The starter course was either a very good house paté or a pancake filled with onions and mushrooms and other delightful local vegetables. Being on the edge of the champagne area they served a little aperitif wine called *ratifia*, which is a stage in the refinement of what finally becomes champagne.

There were several choices for the main dish and I must admit my notes are a bit hazy, but apparently it was very good.

The dining room had round and square tables with white undercloths and brown overcloths, recorded classical music, and quite a few interesting photographs and pewter plates and mugs decorating the walls. The photographs were of various views of the castle, which I could see right outside the window. Dinner is served at seven o'clock.

During my walk I found my way up on the walls of the fortifications where there was a fantastic view of the valley. On my way back to the hotel I discovered a discothèque with lots of colored lights and young people arriving in cars and on motorscooters. So the old France meets the new France.

HOTEL BELLE VUE, Coucy-le-Chateau (Aisne). Tel.: 52-70-12. A castle-hotel set in a small fortified village. Excellent dining room, reasonably priced. Comfortable, somewhat austere bedrooms with washbowl and bidet. No English spoken. Rates: See Index.

Directions: Locate Soissons, northeast of Paris. Coucy-le-Chateau is on the D-1 between Soissons and Chauny. Michelin detailed map 56.

Chantilly

Chantilly is forty-nine kilometers northeast of Paris. It is a city famous for its castle, museum, and beautiful forest, but most of all, for its culinary spécialité: La Crème Chantilly. It is sold at every street corner and lavishly spread on all desserts, so I shall say no more about it. The name of Chantilly is also synonymous with horses: 3,000 horses train here every year and the racetrack is one of the first in France. This equine activity gave birth to another tasty "spécialité": le crottin (literally means horse manure), a goodie made from chocolate, walnuts, and almonds to be found only at Chez M. Richet, maître-patissier, a pastry shop at 45 Rue du Connétable. Just ask for it.

For a description of the castle, better turn to your Michelin Green Guide. *Suffice to say here that its collections make it one of the major museums in France. It is open every day from 10:30 a.m. to 5:00 p.m. except Tuesday. Many other marvels of nature and art are nearby: the ponds of Commelles, the Abbaye de Royaumont— the most beautiful abbey of the Cistercians in this region. The castle grounds, too, are remarkable.*

CHATEAU DE LA TOUR, Gouvieux (Chantilly)

Set in a huge park, it is a large, late 19th-century bourgeois home that boasts, by way of its name, of possessing a tower. I saw no tower, and it is really just a very big, comfortable house. This is precisely what makes it different from other hotels. It has a quiet and warm atmosphere with large, nicely furnished rooms that open onto a labyrinthine corridor.

When I arrived there for lunch, I could tell that something grand was in the making—waitresses and helpers were busily buzzing

around, bringing in more and more plates and flowers and putting out hors d'oeuvres of all descriptions. I stared in wonder…could it be a wedding, could it be a funeral?? I was forgetting that some remarkable youngsters still celebrate their engagements, providing parents and friends with an added opportunity for a banquet. Shortly thereafter, the two little lovebirds floated in, followed by a hungry crowd, and soon the whole dining room resounded with the convivial music of well-fed, happy people.

CHATEAU DE LA TOUR, 60270 Gouvieux (3 km. from Chantilly). Tel. (4) 457-07-39. A 15-guestroom (private baths) typical Norman very large house. Telephones in rooms. Tennis on the property. Horseback riding nearby. Rates: See Index.

Directions: Take D-909 from Chantilly for 3 km, then take first right.

HOSTELLERIE LE GRIFFON, Blérancourt (Aisne)

This rather impressive hotel is a very worthwhile stop on a tour of northern France, and it is even further enhanced by its location on the grounds of Chateau de Blérancourt, a 17th-century mansion that played host to Henry IV and Cardinal Richelieu, and is now the National Museum of Franco-American Friendship.

The museum consists of two wings, one of which illustrates the figures and events that contributed to the development of Franco-

American friendship during the days of Benjamin Franklin and his colleagues in the 18th century. The other wing houses collections relating to artistic, literary, and scentific aspect of Franco-American relations. It also features souvenirs of two World Wars and of volunteer organizations that served in each.

I had no idea there was such a museum and found it a very interesting experience to be walking around the grounds seeing busts of George Washington, John Paul Jones, and Thomas Jefferson, as well as watercolors, line drawings, and maps depicting the cooperation of the French with the American forces during the American Revolution.

How could a hotel in such an atmosphere be anything but superior? When I was there the dining room was being set up for a Sunday brunch and everything looked as if it were running smoothly. I also saw many of the bedrooms and they were quite pleasant, overlooking the little park in front of the chateau as well as the impressive grounds in the rear.

There is some difference in the price of rooms between Le Griffon and the nearby Hotel Belle Vue. This would be my first choice if rooms were available, although the others also turned out to be quite satisfactory.

The hotel is listed in Chateaux Hotels Independants.

HOSTELLERIE LE GRIFFON, 02300 Blérancourt (Aisne). Tel.: (23) 39-60-11. A 26-guestroom impressive hotel with dining room set on the grounds of Chateau de Blérancourt. Open year-round. Closed Sun. night and Mon. Pleasant bedrooms overloking the park and gardens. National Museum of Franco-American Friendship and interesting village for walking. Rates: See Index.

Directions: The village of Chauny is on N-38 about 17 km. from Noyon. Michelin detailed map 56.

ROYAL-CHAMPAGNE, Champillon-Bellevue (Marne)

The signposts directed me to Arras, Cambrai, Amiens, Soissons, and Reims, and although I was not to realize it until later, the next two days had a quality of almost *déjà vu*, feeling as if I had been there before. This might be explained by the fact that as a boy I had grown up with the literature and motion pictures dealing with World War I.

I was certainly far removed from any of the vicissitudes of

conflict as I sat on the terrace of one of the bedrooms of this first of many luxury hotels that are members of the Relais et Chateaux.

I toured many of the bedrooms and there was a definite "decorator" feeling or a kind of studied elegance in each; although the color schemes and patterns were different, all had wallpaper, draperies, and bedspreads to match. Each room had telephone service and a radio—quite a difference from my accommodations at another Belle Vue in Coucy-le-Chateau the previous night. The price was also considerably different as well.

The Relais et Chateaux book classifies this particular accommodation as "comfortable, but simple." To me it seemed a cut or two higher than that. The reception area is quite grand and is decorated with many classic prints of nobility on horseback. The dining room is also designed to overlook the impressive sweep of the valley.

The Royal-Champagne is located near the autoroute between Paris and Metz. It is a very short distance from the great cathedral city of Reims.

ROYAL-CHAMPAGNE (Relais et Chateaux), Champillon-Bellevue (Marne). Tel.: (26) 51-25-06. A luxury hotel in the heart of the champagne country between Paris and Metz, 15 km. from Reims. Bedrooms are elegant with telephones and radios and panoramic views. Rates: See Index.

Directions: Located on N-51 south of Reims en route to Epernay. Michelin detailed map 56.

AUBERGE LA TOURAINE CHAMPENOISE, Tours sur Marne (Marne)

Although I may have mentioned it before, one of the most helpful books for emergency purposes that a visitor in France can possess is called *Logis et Auberges de France,* a guide to a group of small, medium-priced hotels, usually family-run. Not all of them are acceptable. When we come right down to it one of the reasons I'm writing this book is to provide information on acceptable accommodations in all price ranges for a trip to part of France.

Such an accommodation is La Touraine Champenoise, run by the Schosseler family.

I had waited until midafternoon before starting to telephone for accommodations that evening, feeling that May was definitely not the height of the season and that I would have no trouble. Well, I found that even in May it's best to start telephoning earlier and I did see a couple of lodgings in the town of Epernay, which were not at all acceptable. By 5 p.m. I finally made a telephone connection with Madame Schosseler and was delighted to learn that indeed there was a room for me.

This little hotel is typical, but at the same time above standard, of other places I was to see, and has a very pleasant dining room with some good original oils and watercolors. The bedrooms are not very large, but large enough, and some have wc facilities as well as showers.

It is situated on the edge of the Marne Canal and there always seemed to be a barge or boat of some kind in sight. Just a hundred yards on the other side of the canal is the famous river associated with many of the conflicts in this part of France.

As is typical, there were three menus. There was a simple one at the lowest price; the second had three choices; and the third, the most expensive, had six courses.

Madame had fairly good English and with my fairly atrocious French we managed to communicate quite satisfactorily. This would be an excellent stopover for a visit to the champagne country and also the city of Reims.

AUBERGE LA TOURAINE CHAMPENOISE, Tours sur Marne (Marne). Tel.: (26) 59-91-93. A small, typical hotel on the edge of the Marne Canal and close to the Marne River in a calm, peaceful setting. Pleasant dining room and adequate bedrooms, some with private bathrooms. Some English spoken. Closed Jan. 1 to 15. Rates: See Index.

Directions: This is a good place to mention that because of various changes, French maps do not always have the correct road numbers. However, this little village just across the Marne River is located off the Epernay-Chalons road, shown as RD-3 on Michelin map of northern France 998 and detailed map 56. Look for signs on the north side.

Enter now a new character in the dramatis personae—the French Tourist Offices. These offices are located in about fifteen principal cities, and if you're lucky enough to find an office where someone speaks English (if you don't speak adequate French), they can make reservations for you in all parts of France.

HOTEL A LA XII BORNE, Delme (Moselle)

I spent most of the day traveling from near Epernay to Nancy. Part of the trip was alongside the Marne Canal and River with the road leading to several towns of different size, and I realized that the journey was taking much longer than I had anticipated. It had turned quite warm by midafternoon when I arrived in Nancy at the tourist office and discovered that even through it was the beginning of the week and although there was no festival or holiday being celebrated, two of the *logis* I was going to visit could not accommodate me. I threw myself on the mercy of the young woman at the tourist office to see if she could make other arrangements. She made several phone calls and found that everything in the immediate vicinity of Nancy was filled. I finally took the *logis* book and began to choose places at random; we telephoned and between the two of us located this place, just a pleasant drive to the east and north of Nancy.

I arrived at Delme about six o'clock in the evening. The hotel was located on a main street and a busy road to Metz (try to avoid accommodations on the main street or at least get a room in the back of the house).

The town is not located in a particularly scenic area. There are some hills and valleys, but it is not all that exciting.

However, dinner was exceptional. The first dish that caught my eye was the frogs' legs prepared in a Lorraine sauce, the base of which is Riesling wine, reduced to about a tenth of its original volume, and herbs and cream. The result is a real feast—the small frogs' legs were unusually tender and the sauce was good enough to eat with a spoon. I learned that the base of most Lorraine cooking is butter, whereas in some parts of France it is oil, or goose or pork fat. The menu ran to three or four price levels. Among other dishes, there were escargots served in a champagne sauce, coq au vin, and duck l'orange. There was a great deal more to this little hotel than was evident from the exterior, including an extensive dining room and kitchen, and apparently its reputation has spread to several of the nearby urban areas.

Incidentally, it was here that I learned that the French word for the equivalent of "doggie bag" is *picnic demain*, translating literally to "for my picnic tomorrow." On most days I did not stop for lunch at a formal restaurant, there being only so much of this rich, wonderful French food that can be absorbed in a day, so I stopped at various shops, buying cheeses, breads, and fruit, or I asked for a *picnic demain* from the meal the night before.

HOTEL A LA XII BORNE, 57 Delme (Moselle). Tel.: (8) 701-30-18. A 20-room hotel on the main route to Metz, northeast of Nancy, with just adequate bedrooms, none with private bathrooms. The pleasant dining room is superior with an extensive menu. Open all year. Rates: See Index.

Directions: Locate Nancy and then follow N-74 to the junction with D-955 at Chateau-Salins. Delme is on the road between Chateau-Salins and Metz. Michelin detailed map 57.

AUBERGE DU RELAIS DE LA 2eme D.B., Azerailles (Moselle)

I was now on the edge of a considerable holiday and vacation area—the Vosges Mountains, not far from the Rhine River Valley.

The first thing I must point out is that Azerailles is not on Michelin map 998, but it is on Michelin 62 between Luneville and Baccarat, which are on the map. One of the main reasons to visit this part of France is to stop in Luneville, where there is a very pleasant chateau and gorgeous gardens. A dethroned king of Poland, Stanislas, the father-in-law of Louis XV, settled down here and lived his dream of having a quiet and peaceful life. After his passing, the territory of Lorraine was annexed by France, but fortunately the lovely chateau and gardens still remain.

This little hotel was something of a surprise, but I later learned

just how popular this area is for holidays. It sits on the highway right next to a Stella restaurant. There were several very nicely furnished rooms with wallpaper that was also used on the ceiling. The hotel dining room, with several different set meals, was typical.

This hotel is in the *Logis* book and it would make a good overnight stop. I later found still another place that was quite different and was more suitable to my personal taste.

AUBERGE DU RELAIS DE LA 2eme D.B., 54120 Azerailles (Moselle). Tel.: (8) 375-15-01. A 10-room village hotel on the main highway in a popular holiday area near the Vosges Mountains. Most rooms have showers, washbowls, and bidets. Pleasant dining room. Convenient to the Luneville Chateau and gardens. Closed Mon. Rates: See Index.

Directions: This is an area in the Vosges Mountains that is very pleasant for a holiday. It is basically located between Nancy and Strasbourg and there are lots of mountain roads that make excellent back-country driving. This small village is on N-59 between Luneville and Baccarat. Michelin detailed map 62.

GITE ET CHAMBRES D'HÔTES, Azerailles (Moselle)

I stopped out of curiosity and stayed for a part of the morning because this turned out to be a very pleasant place.

The architecture is Alpine and it is obviously a home that has been enlarged to accommodate several guest bedrooms.

There's a distinct German and Swiss flavor about this place with its wood carvings. The central living room, also serving as a dining room, has a large fireplace, and it overlooks a pretty garden in the rear with a barbecue and some children's playthings, like swings and a teeter-totter.

The bedrooms are rather large and there's no commercial feeling about them at all. Most of them seem to have wash basins and lack only one thing to make them most enjoyable—a reading lamp.

Given a choice, I would prefer this place to the small hotel down the road, because it has a much more homelike atmosphere and the proprietors are very cordial. You're literally sharing their home. If this one is not available, the other will do very well.

GITE ET CHAMBRES D'HÔTES, 100 Rue General Leclerc, 54120 Azerailles (Moselle). Tel.: (83) 72-15-15. A 6-guestroom guest house (member of Gite de France) on the main highway in a popular holiday area near the Vosges Mountains. Very pleasant bedrooms, one with private bath, and some with showers. Convenient to the Luneville chateau and gardens. Rates: See Index.

Directions: Azerailles is on N-59 between Luneville and Baccarat. Michelin detailed map 62.

RESIDENCE VOGEL, Heiligenstein

I left Luneville and plunged into the absolutely smashing back roads of the Vosges Mountains. The area between this route and the Wine Road, which winds in and around the east side of the mountains overlooking the Rhine River and Germany beyond, is one of the most highly visited in northern France, and one should never travel during the summer without firm reservations.

It was off-season for me and I decided to stop in Barr, a small town southwest of Strasbourg, and take my chances on getting a room in one of the private residences that are usually available through a tourist office. It was shortly after noon, but even so, it took the young woman quite a few phone calls to track down Madame Vogel.

This was an exceptionally good experience and I would encourage travelers in France to try something like this themselves. If you speak French, call the tourist office in any town and explain that you need a room and bath, or whatever. At a time when there are lots of tourists you'll be glad just to find a room, much less check it out in advance.

Heiligenstein is about two kilometers north of Barr, and the Vogel residence is on a pleasant road at the end of the village. It is a private home nestled among the vineyards and it has a very pretty view of the valley and the Rhine River beyond. It resembled many houses I've seen in Germany, with a broad roof overhanging the front—and this one even had a set of antlers.

Mr. and Mrs. Vogel do not speak English but they do speak German. In this section of France, German is spoken as frequently as French.

There were several different bedrooms from which to choose and all of them were furnished with exceptional taste.

Breakfast was taken on a pleasant little side porch with a partial view of the vineyards. The Vogels and I struggled along in German, French, and English. The conversation wasn't very complicated, but it was a great deal of fun and we did exhange quite a bit of information.

I would recommend staying here if this is the type of accommodation that you prefer, and I must say that it was typical of others in the area.

Later note: I have had several letters from readers commending it.

RESIDENCE VOGEL, 204 Rue Principale, 67140 Heiligenstein. Tel.: (82) 08-94-77. A 3-guestroom guest house in a small village southwest of Strasbourg overlooking the Alsace valley and vineyards. Breakfast included in the price of the room. Convenient as a base for touring the Rhine Valley or the Vosges. English not spoken. Rates: See Index.

Directions: Heiligenstein is on D-35, one of the Wine Roads leading out of Barr. It is not shown on Michelin 998, but is on Michelin detailed maps 62 and 87.

AU RIESLING HOTEL-RESTAURANT, Zellenberg

I had dinner in this restaurant while sharing the table, a customary occurrence at this class of hotel-restaurant, with three other patrons from Bavaria. Our conversation ranged from food and professions to differences among various nationalities. It was a highly enjoyable experience.

The dining room overlooks the fruited plain leading down to the Rhine River. I had a delicious quiche Lorraine that was exceptional. The menu, for about 60 to 150 francs, was interesting and very satisfying. The waitress was an attractive girl with freckles and sparkling black eyes.

I was advised by my new friends to be sure and ask for the regional cheeses as well as the regional wines of France.

My main dish was *coq au Reisling*, chicken cooked in cognac, shallots, Reisling wine, heavy cream, mushrooms, peppers, and fresh parsley. It is browned on top of the stove, flambéd with cognac, then removed, and to the pan are added the shallots, wine, cream and mushrooms, and so forth. When the sauce is smooth the chicken pieces are returned to the pan, covered and cooked for approximately thirty minutes.

The bedrooms are rather plain, but quite adequate, and those in the rear of the house enjoy a view of the valley and the mountains.

AU RIESLING HOTEL-RESTAURANT, 68340 Zellenberg. Tel.: (89) 47-85-85. A very comfortable 36-guestroom restaurant and hotel favored by other middle-class European travelers. Conveniently located to enjoy a stay of one of more days in the Alsatian wine district. Listed in Logis de France. *Rates: See Index.*

Directions: Zellenberg is on a side road between Riquewihr and Ribeauville. It is basically between Selestat and Colmar. Michelin detailed maps 62 and 87.

HOTEL RESTAURANT ARNOLD, Itterswiller

Itterswiller is one of the many lovely villages on the Wine Route, which winds its way through the eastern slopes of the Vosges Mountains.

I was originally attracted to the Arnold because it was situated in a vineyard with a lovely view of the valley and the mountains beyond. It turned out to be a three-star hotel with a little more sophistication than I had found elsewhere—as evidenced in a Christian Dior jewelry display in the lobby.

The rooms were most comfortable, and eight of them had their own balconies overlooking the view of the vineyards and mountains.

The menu included some of the specialties of the region, including wild boar. If you're staying elsewhere in the vicinity this might be
a good place to have dinner, which, at the time of my visit, started at
40 francs.

*HOTEL RESTAURANT ARNOLD, 67140 Ittersiller. Hotel Tel.: (88)
85-51-18; restaurant (88) 85-50-58. A 28-guestroom Wine Route
hotel-restaurant (3 stars) with most impressive views and comfortable
bedrooms. Conveniently located for longer stay in the Alsatian wine
region. Somewhat sophisticated international flavor. Listed in the*
Michelin *and* Logis de France *guides. Rates: See Index.*

*Directions: Itterswiller is in the center of the Alsatian wine country,
446 km. from Paris and 41 km. from Strasbourg. Obtain special Wine
Road map from any tourist office. Also on Michelin detailed maps
62, 87.*

LE CLOS SAINT-VINCENT, Ribeauville

This very impressive accommodation is one of three included in
the Relais et Chateaux group located in the Vosges Mountains and
Rhine Valley area. Because Relais et Chateaux are usually excellent
places to stop, I was doubly regretful at not being able to visit the
other two. One is located in Colroy-la-Roche and the other in
Rouffach. Information about them can be found in the Relais et
Chateaux publication.

I'll always remember this place because of spending two morn-
ings enjoying a breakfast of hot chocolate and fresh croissants on the
balcony of my room overlooking the vineyards in the foreground and
the sweep of the Rhine Valley in the background.

Guest rooms were furnished and decorated with a thought toward creating an atmosphere that would blend well with the beautiful views of the vineyards and the Rhine Valley.

Unfortunately, during the time of my visit the restaurant was
closed, although I did find excellent evening meals nearby. *Michelin*
has awarded Chef Bertrand Chapotin, who is also the owner, one
rosette and lists among the house specialties *ris et rognons de veau
aux petites legumes* (veal sweetbreads and kidney with vegetables)
as well as *filet de turbot a l'oseille.*

*LE CLOS SAINT-VINCENT (Relais et Chateaux), 68150 Ribeauville
(Haut-Rhine). Tel.: (89) 73-67-65. A 9-guestroom luxury accommo-*

dation on a hillside overlooking the Alsatian vineyards and the Rhine River at a distance. Restaurant closed Tues. and Wed. Accommodations available at all times. Open May 1 to mid-Nov. Paris, 429 km.; Colmar, 15 km. Rates: See Index.

Directions: Ribeauville is on the section of the Wine Road which skirts the base of the Vosges Mountains between Selestat and Colmar. Michelin detailed maps 62 and 87.

LE CHALET HOTEL-RESTAURANT, Col de la Schlucht

One of the most interesting and contrasting experiences in the east of France is to take one of the very good roads from Route du Vin over the Vosges Mountains. Following D-417, I stopped at the crest of the mountain in a small village which had a decidedly tourist air, meaning that there was a big parking lot and several restaurants.

I picked one place just on the basis of appearance and because it occurred to me that a traveler coming through here in May might find it a lot of fun to stop and look over the outlook to the east, down a rather precipitous valley toward the Rhine River.

It turned out to be a very pleasant surprise. The innkeeper is a young Frenchman, M. Bouet, who married a Scottish lass, Hazel Bouet, and I chatted with her long enough to find that May is indeed a good time to come here. You can phone from anywhere in France

and make the reservation. It has a sizable restaurant and it is obvious that they do a great many off-the-highway meals.

The somewhat plain bedrooms were quite clean and I would suggest that the bedrooms facing the east would be preferable.

Hazel Bouet, who came originally from Edinburgh, explained that we were about 4,500 feet in altitude and that there were several ski lifts nearby for both downhill and cross-country skiing.

The menu had an emphasis on Alsatian dishes.

The place had a rather bustling but natural feeling, although it could be very busy at certain times of the year. The rates were most appealing (see Index).

LE CHALET HOTEL-RESTAURANT, Col de la Schlucht, 68140 Munster. Tel.: (89) 77-36-44. A hotel-restaurant in a small village at the crest of a mountain, 4,500 feet high, in the Vosges in a tourist area. Clean, plain bedrooms—those facing east recommended. Open year-round. Downhill and xc skiing nearby. English spoken. Rates: See Index.

Directions: Col de la Schlucht is on D-417, one of several roads that cross the Vosges Mountains, which act as a natural shelter for the Rhine River valley. The area is criss-crossed with many delightful back roads. There are dozens of ways to go from point to point. See Michelin detailed maps 62 and 87.

DES BAS RUPTS HOTEL-RESTAURANT, Gerardmer

You just never know what you're going to find in France. At first I thought this hotel was a Bavarian nightmare with a sort of pseudo-contemporary facade. At least ten badges of acceptance were at the front door and it is also listed in the *Logis de France*. It's one of the few members of Relais du Silence, an organization devoted to the maintenance of tranquil accommodations. I cannot on such a short visit judge its tranquility.

In the reception area I saw a handsome man in a chef's outfit who turned out to be Michel Philippe, who could very well be a star of television and cinema. Furthermore, he was quite versed in English and I happened to catch him at a time when the kitchen was not that busy.

I toured almost all of the guest rooms and most of them were furnished in contemporary Scandinavian, one or two had classic furnishings. The rooms in the back have a very close view of the mountains and those in the front are larger with a more pleasant view.

At lunch, I had my first taste of noisettes of wild boar, which was served with two different sauces. Also, on a most attractively arranged plate was a small mashed potato ball, which had been dipped in egg, rolled in slivered almonds, and either baked or fried. These are called *pommes almonds* and they are served with very thin french-cut green beans and baby carrots with their tops on. Lunch was completed with some Muenster cheese. I agree that Monsieur Philippe deserves all of the honors and diplomas that are hanging in the reception area.

I would also give this place the Berkshire Traveller four-star rating for having the most elegant public toilets I have ever seen. There was carpeting on the floor and a sort of common wash-up room shared by both men and women—the theme is Art Deco all the way.

Michelin lists Bas Rupts as a top-class restaurant with one rosette. Since this is a resort area, there are also several places nearby.

DES BAS RUPTS HOTEL-RESTAURANT, 88400 Gerardmer (Vosges). Tel.: (29) 63-09-25; Telex: 960-992. A 19-guestroom mountain hotel-restaurant with many citations and memberships; also a Relais du Silence. All bedrooms have private baths; rooms in front preferable. Tennis, school for xc skiing close by; downhill ski area 2 km. Rates: See Index.

Directions: Gerardmer is also on D-489 which runs across the Vosges Mountains, beginning I believe at Chaumont and ending in Colmar. Michelin detailed maps 62, 87.

HOTEL DE FRANCE, Luxeuil-les-Bains

Here is a hotel about as French as you can find. It needs only such literary figures of the twenties as Hemingway and F. Scott Fitzgerald to complete the picture. The stairways go "this-away" and "that-away" and there are all kinds of French newspapers and posters. It has the feeling of a stage setting for the *Madwoman of Chaillot*. It is a scene that one of the French impressionists might have sketched. The building itself is white, with balconies on the front and gardens along one side.

The big reason to come to this town is to "take the waters," and the Hotel de France, as well as the other establishments, caters to travelers who are so disposed. There are several little parks in town and it is not at all the kind of place that would be on a tour arranged by your friendly local travel agency.

Meals are offered, but I was just passing through, so I missed the pleasure.

I did look at a couple of other accommodations in the town, but this seemed to be the one that appealed to me the most. It had a very natural feeling.

HOTEL DE FRANCE, 6 Rue Georges-Clemenceau, 70300 Luxeuil-les-Bains. Tel.: (84) 40-13-90. A 20-guestroom hotel with gardens on the edge of a small, interesting town known for its mineral baths. Atmosphere reminiscent of the twenties; furnishings somewhat austere. Some rooms with private baths. Meals offered. Open year-round. Tennis court, park nearby. Rates: See Index.

Directions: This would be a good stop en route to or from the Rhine River valley. Luxeuil-les-Bains is roughly between Besançon to the south and Nancy to the north. It is south of Epinal. Luxeuil is a larger town than I had expected. At the crossroads in the middle of town, take the road north to the bath areas and look for Rue Georges-Clemenceau. Michelin detailed map 66.

LE RELAIS DE NANTILLY, Nantilly

It had been a very interesting day that started at Le Clos Saint Vincent in Ribeauville in the valley of the Rhine. The road had taken me across the crest of the Vosges Mountains to Gerardmer and into Luxeuil, the city of the baths. I deliberately chose to follow the yellow roads on my Michelin map of northern France (998) instead of following the usually more-traveled roads printed in red.

The trip was well worth the trouble as it led through a somewhat unspoiled and natural part of France with beautiful views of the countryside. It was so unspoiled that I looked in vain for signs of small hotels or inns that I might include in this book, but to my dismay I found none. It just wasn't a road that an ordinary tourist would choose.

I had made reservations at Le Relais de Nantilly, so I felt fairly safe in arriving about six o'clock in the evening, knowing that my reservation had been confirmed and that I would have a good dinner and a comfortable bedroom.

This is a lovely chateau surrounded by generous fields and

parklands. It's quite typical of some of the middle-sized chateaux that I saw during my two trips to France. The original use was probably by a well-to-do family of the 18th century, and most of the bedrooms were quite large with excellent views of the countryside and all had modern bathroom facilities.

The dining room here was surprisingly small, which I think made it more cozy. Several interesting watercolors adorned the walls. The service was very agreeable and quite informal. A man whom I took to be the manager or even one of the proprietors was also the headwaiter, and the rather attractive woman at the front desk turned out to be his wife, who also assisted in the dining room service. The atmosphere was like that of many American country inns owned by husband-and-wife teams.

The dinner was most enjoyable. I had some langoustinos in a special cheese sauce that was so delicious I surreptitiously dipped my bread in to soak up all of it. The remainder of the menu had typical French dishes. I chose an enticing dessert from a center table decorated with fresh roses.

The morning was very pleasant with guests enjoying a cup of coffee and warm croissants at the bar. I think we were all relieved to find that the all-night rain had stopped and we had a fresh, sunshiny morning in which to start another day.

This little chateau was very pleasant and had one quality that I found quite indispensable—it was very quiet.

LE RELAIS DE NANTILLY (Relais et Chateaux), Nantilly, 70100 Gray. Tel.: (84) 65-20-12. A 26-guestroom chateau-hotel surrounded by park and woods in a quiet, unspoiled countryside. A small and informal but excellent dining room. Large bedrooms with modern baths and telephones. Rates: See Index.

Directions: You'll definitely need Michelin 998 (northern France) to locate this place. Locate Dijon and follow D-70 toward Gray. Note D-2, a secondary road leading to Autrey. The Relais is on D-2. Michelin detailed map 66.

CHATEAU DE FLEURVILLE, Fleurville (Saône-et-Loire)

Leaving my very pleasant accommodations at Nantilly, I followed D-70 to Dijon, then N-74 south to Beaune and Chalon, which for a few miles would duplicate the route of my earlier journey, and finally N-6, the road from Paris to Marseille.

Noting a reference to Chateau de Fleurville at this point, I decided to leave the motorway and seek it out.

The chateau was built in the 1600s and apparently was remodeled a few hundred years later. It is quite a distance off the highway in a setting of forests and fields. The beautiful beige-tinted stone walls, gray shutters, ivy-covered round turrets, and stained glass windows with their coat of arms lend an air of authentic antiquity.

The entrance is through a massive wood door into a hallway and staircase with at least seven different mounted deer heads leading to the second floor. This baronial theme extends to most of the bedrooms, which have canopy beds and elaborately carved armoires.

The menus seemed to be reasonable at 100 to 200 francs.

The rather imposing Frenchwoman who seemed to be in charge did not speak English, but I did learn that the restaurant was not open on Mondays. However, accommodations were available.

There are quite a few of these chateaux being restored and converted into hotels in France, and this one seemed to be a good value for the money. The atmosphere is very ancient and pleasant and it is just a few miles from the wine centers of Mâcon. *Michelin* rates it as a "pleasant hotel with an interesting view." I agree.

CHATEAU DE FLEURVILLE, 71260 Fleurville (Saône-et-Loire). Tel.: (85) 33-12-17. An 11-guestroom 17th-century chateau in Saône River

valley, at the foot of the vineyards of Mâcon. All bedrooms have
private baths. Dining room is closed on Mon. No English spoken.
Rates: See Index.

Directions: I'm sorry to say that Fleurville is so small that it is not even
listed on Michelin 999 (southern France). It is located to the north of
Mâcon between N-6 and A-6. If on A-6 use either Mâcon North or
Tournus exit.

HOTEL-RESTAURANT DE LA PLACE, Polliat

At Mâcon I left the N-6 and headed east on N-79 toward Bourg
and the French Alps at Annecy. However, en route I stopped at this
very pleasant little town and decided to include this hotel and
restaurant as typical of many of its type available in France. It is listed
in the *Logis* book, and *Michelin* gives it a rather humble rating:
"plain, but adequate hotel." I found it to be tremendously interesting
and particularly enjoyed myself. It is not very likely that you'll run
into very many other Americans or Europeans, either at dinner or as
overnight guests. It is a place, in the words of James Thurber, where
"truck drivers stop."

Located about 400 yards off the main road on a small parking
plaza, it is far enough away from the truck traffic to be relatively
undisturbed at night.

The first floor of the building contains a busy restaurant, a busy
bar, and a busy bakery. I had to make a few halting inquiries in
English finally to get the right person to show me the bedrooms,
which were plain but serviceable and, above all, clean.

There's really no check-in desk. After locating the waitress-
clerk, I followed her through the back of the dining room to an
outside back stairway that led up to a pleasant little guest balcony,
and on to several different bedrooms.

I would encourage the reader to feel free to seek accommodations of this type as well as those of a more elegant nature. I think
travelers to France discover early on that the cost of the meal does not
necessarily indicate the amount of enjoyment to be derived from it.
For instance, this is far from an elegant restaurant, but there were
tablecloths and the least expensive menu included a soufflé as well
as selections of eels, trout amandine, grilled lamb chops, and a
quarter of roast chicken. There were eleven main dishes along with

vegetables, cheese, and dessert. It was one of the best values for the money I found in France and it was certainly a great deal better than some that would cost three or four times as much. At the far side of the dining room was a group of posters advertising motocross and shooting contests.

I was given a tour of the very busy kitchen and it was the equal of many that I visited where the menus were far more expensive.

This is a good place for me to explode the myth about Americans not being accepted in France or that the French always refuse to speak English, resenting visitors. I received very affable nods and greetings from truck drivers and motorcyclists of both genders and nobody thought it strange that I was talking into my tape recorder all the time.

So if I arrived here about eight o'clock at night, I'd welcome the opportunity for a quiet bedroom and a reasonably priced meal; if I were traveling with children, I'd think that it was exceptional.

It's interesting to note that this village is just a few minutes from one of the great restaurants in France, La Mere Blanc, praised elsewhere in this book. I might say that Monsieur George Blanc, who has the coveted three stars from *Michelin*, is himself a very humble man and I wouldn't have been surprised to find him partaking of the noon meal at the Hotel de la Place. La Mere Blanc enjoys a deserved reputation in France, but the Hotel de la Place has its own little niche.

HOTEL-RESTAURANT DE LA PLACE, 01310 Polliat. Tel.: (74) 30-40-19. A 10-guestroom small but busy, typically French hotel-restaurant just off the main highway in a pleasant town. Bedrooms are clean and adequate. Restaurant offers a good selection at very reasonable prices. Closed 3 wks. in June. Rates: See Index.

Directions: Polliat is just another wide place in the road and not identified on Michelin 999 (southern France). However, it is on N-79 about 10 km. west of Bourg.

HOTEL DE L'ABBAYE, Talloires (Haut Savoie)

It was, as one of the guests who joined me briefly at the table on the terrace in front of the Hotel de L'Abbaye said, *"Il fait beau."* Even if I had forgotten that this French phrase meant "A beautiful day," I would certainly have gotten his meaning, because the gorgeous sunlight was sparkling on the lake waters, not more than twenty yards in front of us, against the green backdrop of mountains that seemed to plunge into the lakeside. Fluffy clouds overhead played hide and seek.

It was the calm end of a day that had started north of Dijon and involved a very spectacular ride over the mountains from Bourg to Nantua and beyond. I was feeling particularly fortunate that I had stumbled into this section of France. Although it is located on the edge of the French Alps (Mont Blanc, as well as the ski resorts, is just a few miles away) it is not on the general route of the first-time traveler to France.

Hotel de L'Abbaye, a member of the Relais group, had much to recommend it. For one thing it has a most interesting history that became evident as soon as I walked through the rather austere front entrance. The building was built as a priory in the 11th century and for six centuries was very rich, thanks to gifts from the bishops and counts of Geneve and the dukes of Savoie. In 1674 it became a royal abbey but fell into disrepair because the monks, who were really feudal lords of the time, were more interested in the delights of the flesh than in spiritual atonement. The French Revolution saw the Benedictine Abbey destroyed.

Today, it is a very pleasant and modern hotel enjoying an unsurpassed view of Lake Annecy and the mountains. Above all, it is beautifully calm and quiet.

Another attractive feature for me personally is the fact that it is run by a family, and part of my information was gathered during an interesting talk with the father of the present innkeeper, who beguiled me with some fascinating facts, not only about the hotel but also about the surrounding area.

I remained at the Hotel de L'Abbaye for two nights, partly because it was one of the most enchanting of all holiday experiences and partly because the village also is the location of one of the very few three-star restaurants in France: L'Auberge du Pere Bise, about which I will report directly.

HOTEL DE L'ABBAYE (Relais et Chateaux), 74290 Talloires (Haut Savoie). Tel.: (50) 67-40-88. A 34-guestroom hotel, originally an 11th-century priory on the shore of Lake Annecy in the scenic Savoie district. Open May 1 to Oct. 10. All bedrooms have private baths. À la carte menu. Tennis, golf, boating, beautiful walks, and backroading. Rates: See Index.

Directions: I drove from Mâcon east to Bourg and then followed D-979 to Nantua and Bellegarde (N-84). This section is part of the truck route from Lyon to Geneve. The trucks go on to Switzerland at Bellegarde and the road becomes driveable into Annecy (N-508). An alternate road would be to continue to pick up the main autoroute from Lyon to Annecy. At Annecy follow the roads to Geneve, but keep your eye peeled to the right for the road to Thone. This road passes down the east side of the lake and there will be an arrow pointing toward Talloires at that point. It is the only way to get there. Once in the village point your car toward the lakeshore. Good luck. Michelin detailed map 92.

Further Notes on French Cuisine

I've always considered myself more a chronicler of people and ambience than an expert on cuisine. I prefer to leave food critiques to my peers in the travel-writing world, and as I have remarked several times in this and other books, I am by choice an almost-teetotaller. Oh, I've sampled the wines in various sections of Europe with what I call a "sacrificial sip," but you'll find no knowledgeable, gustatory phrases flowing from my pen. By the way, it's possible to travel all over Europe and not feel that it is necessary to drink the wine if you would prefer to abstain. The bottled mineral water is very satisfactory and does not interfere with relishing the truly unusual and excellent food. For years an old wives' tale has been circulated (by the vintners) that the water in certain European countries is literally undrinkable and it is necessary to drink wine everywhere in self defense. It is also untrue that headwaiters in great French restaurants are offended if wine is not ordered with the meal. The fact is a great many Europeans do not take wine with their meals. I encourage the reader to follow whatever course of action pleases him or her, and not to be concerned about the so-called customs of the country. No one really cares.

Having disavowed myself of any expertise in the food and wine department, I will say that I have been tremendously pleased at all categories of European restaurants, from the simple to the three-star. I think there is a generous sampling of various levels of cuisine in this book and I approach the subject with a typical American palate and admiration for a good meal.

L'AUBERGE DU PÈRE BISE, Talloires (Haut Savoie)

A visitor to Talloires ought to spend at least two nights there, of which one would be spent dining at Père Bise. I might add that I had my other evening meal at Hotel L'Abbaye and found it to be excellent.

Because of its reputation as one of the twenty-one or so *Michelin* three-star restaurants in France, it would be quite easy to be intimidated by Père Bise before ever entering its door. It is located on one of the points of land that jut out into Lake Annecy, and it has a beautiful terrace that is especially inviting on warm afternoons and evenings, although dinner is actually served inside the restaurant.

The menu, which has several courses, really is dedicated to quite simple preparations of regional produce and is further enhanced by the fresh-water fish from the lake. The fruits and berries as well as the cheeses of the region are excellent. It is well to inquire about the local cheeses, as some of them are different and very satisfying. The cuisine is in the classic French style and the choices should include *l'omble chevalier*, the fish from the lake.

The dinner menu runs about $100 and allows a choice of several different dishes. It's also possible to order à la carte, but as nearly as I can determine it is still an expensive experience. The menu is changed almost daily and I would suggest that almost anything would be satisfactory. Remember to save some space for a selection from the dessert cart. A superb dessert is the *marjolaine*, a seven-layered chocolate dessert, that makes me almost perish with joy when I think of it.

Oddly enough, the same lake fish is also served at the rather simple restaurants in the village.

L'AUBERGE DU PÈRE BISE (Relais et Chateaux), 74290 Talloires (Haut Savoie). Tel.: (50) 60-72-01. Michelin 3-star restaurant on the shores of Lake Annecy. Classic French cuisine, with both full-course and à la carte menus. Rates: See Index.

Directions: Follow directions as given for Hotel de L'Abbaye. Michelin detailed map 92.

LA TOUR DE PACORET, Grésy-sur-Isère (Savoie)

What a wonderful day! I reluctantly left the Hotel de L'Abbaye in Talloires on the shores of Lake Annecy and headed in a southerly direction on N-90 between Albertville and Chambery. To the east the

towering snowcaps of the French Alps soared into the blue sky. The road ran beside a rushing river with small farms on both sides of the valley. Ahead was a sign for an auberge, and out of some sixth sense I decided to turn off, wishfully thinking perhaps I might find that ideal, out-of- the-way French inn that no one had ever visited before, run by bilingual, gracious French people who couldn't do enough for their guests.

Would you believe that La Tour de Pacoret was almost perfect.

In the first place, the setting in the mountains of Savoie is breathtaking. It is a 14th-century watchtower that was the former residence of the counts of Pacoret. The tower has had later additions to it and I'm sure the original counts lived in simple luxury.

The views from all of the guest rooms are impressive. All the rooms have carved beds, armoires, original oils, and private wc's. The rooms are named after flowers, of which the area has an abundance.

One of the focal points is a delightful terrace that enjoys a panoramic view of the mountains. This beautiful view is also shared by the dining room.

The longer I stayed, the more enchanted I became and I was also delighted to learn that a very pleasant lunch was served as well as dinner. This is one of the wine regions of France and the countryside, as in Alsace, also has a typical Route de Vin.

This little gem is also in *Michelin,* and as a Relais du Silence has received very good marks, particularly for being quiet and secluded. The owner is a sophisticated Frenchwoman and it is obvious that her taste is the dominant influence in the furnishings and decor.

Now don't tell anybody I told you about this place. It will be our secret. (I did tell two dear friends, Janet and Ruth Pinkham. They adored it.)

LA TOUR DE PACORET, Grésy-sur-Isère, 73460 Frontenex (Savoie). Tel.: (79) 37-91-59. A secluded former 14th-century watchtower, now a 2-star hotel-restaurant in the midst of breathtaking scenery in the Savoie district. All bedroms have private baths and impressive views. Closed Dec., Jan., & Feb. Dining room offers lunch as well as dinner. Rates: See Index.

Directions: The main road between Albertville and Chambery has two designations: N-90, which leads on into the high mountains and the St. Bernard pass, and N-6. Grésy is a small village on D-201, about 4 km. to the northwest, running parallel to the main road. La Tour de Pacoret is well signposted. Michelin detailed map 92.

LE LIEVRE AMOUREUX, Saint-Lattier (Isère)

Le Lievre Amoureux is distinctly French. In many places in France efforts are made by proprietors of various establishments to cater to an international patronage. Here, I found few concessions to travelers from America or any other country.

I'll confess that I had a very difficult time communicating, although it wasn't because the owner, a very attractive French-woman, wasn't cordial. Her English was about equal to my French, so some of my questions went unanswered.

The exterior of the main building is quite attractive, although I was disappointed to find that there were apparently very few bed-rooms available in it, and I spent the night in a nearby building that was a sort of annex. Just a few miles away there is an additional building that is a kind of hillside cottage.

An interesting feature is the fact that guests can look through windows down into a spotless kitchen were brigades of chefs and under-chefs wearing the whitest uniforms imaginable, move about among copper utensils that are burnished to a fare-thee-well.

I gathered that the reputation of the restaurant is considerable. *Michelin* classifies it as "very comfortable" and awards it one rosette. It certainly had a very attractive appearance and the menu was quite extensive. I'll confess that having dined at Père Bise the previous night (rather expensively) that I was not in the mood for another high-priced meal and the story of my evening repast is told in the next section. I try to find accommodations and restaurants for this book in a wide range of prices so that the reader/traveler may have a choice.

The English translation of the name of this small inn is "the amorous hare" and in the lounge there is a handsome oil painting of two of this species doing a mating dance in the woods.

LE LIEVRE AMOUREUX (Relais et Chateaux), Saint-Lattier, 38160 Saint Marcellin (Isère). Tel.: (76) 36-50-67. A restaurant-hotel in a village near the French Alps. Some guestrooms in main building; others in nearby buildings. Bedrooms quite austere. Restaurant has a considerable reputation. Ski area within 20 km. Rates: See Index.

Directions: Saint-Marcellin is off N-92, which runs between Romans and Moirans. This is an area northwest of Grenoble. The map is a great deal more confusing than the actual area itself, so don't be dismayed. Detailed map 93.

AUBERGE DU VIADUC RESTAURANT, Saint-Lattier (Isère)

If this place only had bedrooms I would classify it as the kind of a find that I made a few pages ago at La Tour de Pacoret. However, much to my dismay it is only a restaurant.

This turned out to be one of my most enjoyable meals in France. Each dish was individually prepared and brought out in the dish in which it was cooked. There were fresh flowers on the table and a discreet little lamp. Other patrons were an assortment of French people enjoying a Saturday night dinner.

Among the things I remember about the inexpensive menu is rabbit with a delicious sauce, salmon served in a purée of spinach and herbs. The first course was fresh asparagus with another delightful sauce. (France is a land of sauces.)

The meal finished off with a big cheese selection and then, for a small restaurant, the world's largest collection of desserts on what the proprietors call a dessert chariot. Other guests had small portions of two or three varieties. I contented myself with the caramel custard, but the orange ice cream loaf looked excellent and so did the creamy tutti frutti cake.

I was delighted to reaffirm my faith in *Michelin* by noting that this humble restaurant was listed as a "very comfortable restaurant."

The service was simple, with the same waitress who took the order also serving it. The proprietors were most cordial and there was a very pleasant, informal atmosphere. Although I dislike eating good meals all by myself, I must say the cordiality in the dining room made up for it. If you're traveling between Chambery and Valence by way of Grenoble, stick to the motorways, particularly through Grenoble. Once out in the country the side roads are delightful.

AUBERGE DU VIADUC RESTAURANT, 38840 Saint-Lattier (Isère). Tel.: (76) 36-51-65. A chef-owned, small but excellent restaurant with a pleasant, informal atmosphere.

Directions: Saint-Lattier is on N-92 just northeast of Romans. Look for the restaurant adjacent to the viaduct. Detailed map 93.

LA VIEILLE AUBERGE, Charmes en Ardèche

After an interval of a few years I once again drove down the N-86 from Lyon toward Avignon. The sun was shining, the day was fair, and after the success of finding such an exceptional restaurant on the previous night, I fully expected to discover some outstanding inns and small hotels today.

As I passed by a small village on the west bank of the Rhone, I noted a sign indicating that La Vieille Auberge, the village inn, was located just a short distance from the highway. I turned into the village and after negotiating some rather pleasant but narrow streets, spotted the front entrance to the inn and pulled into a convenient parking space, sometimes a problem in European towns.

What a delight this inn proved to be! It has a very attractive tiny reception area and was flanked on the right by a dining room with a low vaulted ceiling. Since it was late May, an ancient fireplace was filled with fresh flowers. The rough walls were adorned with tapestries, and I've never seen tablecloths any whiter.

Although the staff was in the midst of scrubbing down the hallways and cleaning the rooms, one young man who seemed to be more or less in charge was delighted to show me a few of the bedrooms and explain the items on the menu.

I was very pleased with the bedrooms. They all had wc's and, even though this was a building dating back to the 16th century that had probably seen several different uses, they were of a very comfortable size. Some of the rooms looked out into a little courtyard and others had a view of the colorful roofs of the village.

The menu had several local specialties and I learned that the chef was also the owner of this little village inn, which would have been quite in place in many parts of North America.

This would be an ideal stop for anyone traveling north or south from Avignon or Marseille. Prices (see Index) are relatively modest and I would imagine that the rooms are quiet. If the cuisine is half as palatable as the appearance of the dining room, all should be well. It was only after I left that I discovered that it was listed in both *Michelin*, which rated it as a "comfortable restaurant," and the *Logis* guide to hotels.

LA VIEILLE AUBERGE, 07800 Charmes-sur-Rhone, Ardèche. Tel.: (75) 60-80-10. A chef-owned small village inn-restaurant in a 16th-century building in the Ardèche area near the Rhone River. Bedrooms have private baths and telephones. Restaurant offers breakfast, lunch, and dinner; closed Wed. and Sun. eves. Rates: See Index.

Directions: This village is not shown on Michelin 999 (southern France); however, it is just a few km. south of Valence on N-86, which parallels the Rhone River on the west side. The N-7 and A-7 run parallel to the river on the east side and there are convenient exits and a bridge crossing opposite Charmes.

HOSTELLERIE DU CHATEAU DE CUBIERES, Roquemaure (Gard)

I believe that I have mentioned a small booklet, obtainable at member hotels, entitled *Chateaux Hotels Independants*. While traveling through France I referred to this book frequently to make certain that I was not passing up anything that might be worth seeing. Most of the places in it are concentrated in the north-central section of France and the wine country. However, there are a few in the area near Avignon and Nimes. It was for that reason I left the autoroute at Orange after some inquiries and made my way to Roquemaure to visit this chateau. This area is shown on Michelin 80 and 81.

It turned out to be well worth the trip. The basic house is a three-story, 18th-century chateau with rather extensive gardens, and obviously was the residence of rather affluent owners at various times during the past. It is in the outskirts of the village and is set in a small park at a sufficient distance from the road to make it rather quiet.

The main entrance is through a large door into a spacious hallway with much emphasis on Roman architecture. A sweeping marble staircase leads to the second floor and the bedrooms are high-ceilinged and furnished with heavy wooden bedsteads, armoires, and other quite attractive pieces, with good reading lamps. The view overlooks the park and lawns, where there were some palm trees mixed in with the evergreens.

There's a sort of rumpled air about the chateau that doesn't detract from it in the slightest. *Michelin* terms it "comfortable."

On the day of my visit there was a wedding party in the restaurant, a separate building that was once a barn or storehouse with a very pleasant outside terrace. Even though the party was rather gay and lively, a young baby slept in its traveling crib throughout all the merriment.

I think this would be an excellent place to stop for a couple of days to tour the towns of Avignon, Nimes, and even Arles. It's not de luxe and it's not a youth hostel, but it's somewhere in-between. It seemed to be a reasonable place to stay and a good value.

HOSTELLERIE DU CHATEAU DE CUBIERES, Roquemaure (Gard). Tel.: (66) 50-14-28. An 18th-century chateau-hotel in a park on the outskirts of a small village near Avignon. All bedrooms have private bathrooms. Restaurant in separate building. Closed Feb. 20 to Mar. 20 and Nov. 15 to 30. Rates: See Index.

Directions: The key to finding this hotel is to locate Roquemaure on the map first. If on N-7, use the Orange exit. If coming south on N-86, turn southeast at Bagnols following Route N-580 and look for signs to Roquemaure. Many times it's easier to follow roads leading to specific towns rather than using route numbers that have a way of changing. Michelin detailed map 81.

LES FRÊNES HOTEL, Avignon-Montfavet

It was very quiet in Avignon-Montfavet. Only the sounds of birds interrupted this sublime quietude as I stretched on a deck chair beside a swimming pool at Les Frênes Hotel. The warm afternoon sun of Provence was lulling me into a delicious lassitude and I realized that this was one of the few times on my second excursion through France that I had actually taken the time to act like a vacationer.

I leafed through a small guidebook outlining the historic and cultural sites and palaces of the city, preparatory to a visit in the early evening. I had barely had time a few years earlier to see the Papal Palace and other truly impressive landmarks within this walled city.

Les Frênes was a perfect setting for a few hours in the sunshine. It's an elegant small hotel, built in the early part of the 19th century and artfully located in a park with expansive lawns, very beautiful gardens, and swaying trees that in May were in full leaf. There were two swimming pools, one for children and one for adults.

Guest rooms are for the most part in small individual apartments and in addition to being very tastefully decorated, all have private bathrooms, color television, and directly connected telephones.

The dining room and a most comfortable parlor are in the main building. It's the kind of atmosphere that invites the traveler to enjoy the rather sumptuous surroundings, including some good, original, palette-knife paintings. The proprietress, Mme. Biancone, takes the orders and the guests are seated when the first course is ready. The dining room looks out over the park past the swimming pools.

The menu is à la carte and, as I remarked several times, it is sometimes easier in France to choose from the à la carte menu. Since I had eaten rather handsomely at noon, I decided to have a single course and perhaps a dessert—French desserts are very difficult to refuse.

It's quite easy to reach the center of Avignon, and I'm happy to say I enjoyed a most agreeable evening in the moonlight of Provence.

Earlier, I had enjoyed a very pleasant reunion with Jacques

Mille, the owner of the Hostellerie Le Prieuré in Villeneuve-les-Avignon, a few miles away to the west of Avignon, just as Montfavet is more or less to the southeast (see Itinerary Number One). These two accommodations provide an interesting contrast, and the reader may choose between Les Frênes, where the only activity is a swimming pool, and Le Prieuré, where there are many more rooms, several tennis courts, and a more cosmopolitan atmosphere.

LES FRÊNES HOTEL (Relais et Chateaux), Avenue des Vertes Rives, 84140 Avignon-Montfavet. Tel.: (90) 31-17-93. A 15-guestroom 19th-century hotel set in a park, 7 min. from Avignon. All bedrooms have private bathrooms, telephones, and TV. À la carte dining room. Swimming pool. Rates: See Index.

Directions: Follow the ring road around Avignon and take the turn-off for Montfavet, on the right after the turn-off for Marseille.

LE MAS D'AIGRET, Les Baux de Provence

After a very pleasant visit and lunch with M. Lalleman at L'Auberge de Noves (see Itinerary Number One). I was now headed across the French countryside toward Arles.

The character of the countryside changed quite abruptly from the gentle fields and farms outside of Noves to a more rugged landscape that reminded me of the Canary Islands, and also, oddly enough, parts of Arizona. The main road curved around some rock formations covered with a scrubby bush. The feeling was the same as being in a desert; there were very few houses and even fewer people.

Up ahead, however, was a massive rock formation—first only a silhouette—but then as I got closer I could see that it resembled castle walls. As I got even closer I decided that if it were indeed a castle, it was one of the largest I had ever seen.

So engrossed was I with this really formidable rock pile that I almost missed the sign for the hotel Le Mas d'Aigret, painted on one of the dun-colored boulders beside the road. I sensed a new adventure and pulled into the parking lot, but this was accompanied by a twinge of misgiving, as I wasn't particularly impressed with the appearance of the hotel from the outside. In fact, I left the motor running, feeling that I would just take a quick look around and probably be on my way.

I opened the wooden door, stepped into the lobby and reception area, and immediately ran outside, turned off the motor, and thus

began a most agreeable visit that was rewarding in every possible way.

To begin with, although the main house is a conventional, Mediterranean-type building, it is actually built up against sheer rock, and a great deal of the hotel, including the dining room and some of the bedrooms, has been carved out of granite. This is particularly noticeable in the dining room and lounge area, where the walls have some extremely interesting palette-knife oils that blend very well with the texture of the rock. There is a marvelous fireplace in one end of the cave that, on a slightly cool May afternoon, had a very pleasant fire.

I was getting a great feeling from the entire place and this was strengthened when I met the members of the innkeeping family, one of whom was an attractive French girl who had lived for a short time in the United States. She was wearing a blue denim skirt and a green T-shirt, and she had a touch of the French panache that was echoed in the sophisticated informality of the hotel. From her I learned that the nearby castle was indeed an ancient city and one of the most sought-out tourist objectives in this part of France. Later on in the afternoon I spent a couple of hours wandering around the battlements and narrow streets.

She showed me a copy of the April, 1981, *House Beautiful* with a whole section on Provence, including a dissertation on the cooking, the architecture, the painting, and, among other things, a beautiful photograph of the terrace of the hotel.

I noticed that just a few miles away is one of the most prestigious accommodations in all of France (another surprise).

But I must say I found the atmosphere and the hospitality of the proprietors here extremely appealing. *Michelin* gives it two red turrets (I'm not sure what that means). I would certainly give it good marks for location, congeniality, and friendliness.

LE MAS D'AIGRET, 13520 Les Baux de Provence. Tel.: (90) 97-33-54. An unusual and pleasant small hotel in the foothills at the base of ruins of a remarkable castle-city. Rooms are in three buildings, all with private bathrooms, and many with views. Dining room serves breakfast and dinner. Swimming pool. Rates: See Index.

Directions: Because Les Baux is a well-known tourist objective, it is very plainly marked on all French maps between Arles and Avignon.

OUSTAU DE BAUMANIÈRE, Les Baux de Provence

This is one of the great places to eat in France. It's about ten or fifteen minutes from the previous hotel mentioned and *Michelin* has awarded it five red crossed spoons and forks and three rosettes. I understand there are only five or six other restaurants in France to receive this highly desirable rating.

At the time of my visit, bookings for the evening meal were closed, but since I've never considered myself a particularly astute critic of food to begin with, I felt the only loss was the opportunity to enjoy what I'm sure would have been an exceptional meal. Incidentally, the menu is à la carte.

The location is most unusual because it enjoys a full view of some more of the rocky fortifications of the village of Les Baux de Provence and it is surrounded by beautiful formal gardens and a lovely reflecting pool. Where Le Mas d'Aigret sits up high, overlooking a valley, Oustau de Baumanière is set in its own box canyon, surrounded by pinnacles of limestone that have eroded over countless centuries. I hadn't really planned to stop here, and I arrived much too late in the day to feel comfortable about asking the assistant manager at the reception area to take time from a busy checking-in session with newly arrived guests to show me any of the rooms. Actually, I was booked for the night a few kilometers away, but this was a surprise discovery.

However, let me hasten to add that I feel very good about including it in this book. Even without having a meal or staying overnight, it has the unmistakable signs of good taste and discrimination. It might be a bit pricey for some travelers, but there are many who will undoubtedly agree that it's worth it. The parking lot was filled with Mercedes Benzes and Peugots. There were also a couple of vintage Rolls Royces.

OUSTAU DE BAUMANIÈRE (Relais et Chateaux), Les Baux de Provence, 13520 Maussane les Apilles. Tel.: (90) 97-33-07. Telex: 420203 Baucabro. A luxury hotel- restaurant set in a small canyon at the foot of limestone cliffs. Bedrooms are in several buildings and have private bathrooms and telephones. Tennis, swimming pool, horseback riding on grounds. Rates: See Index.

Directions: Locate Les Baux in the area south of Avignon and north of Arles. I recommend following the roads printed in yellow on Michelin 999 (southern France). Detailed map 83.

LA REGALIDO, Fontvieille

Chef-owner Jean-Pierre Michel had just returned from the fish market and he whipped the cover off his market basket like a magician to show us some big, beautiful sea bass. "I prepare like a filet of sole and then slice the way you would a smoked salmon," he said. "It is one of our most popular main dishes."

The invitation to come into the kitchen of this lovely little inn a few miles outside of Arles was an indication of its genuinely friendly spirit. I don't believe I've been invited to visit more than three other French kitchens and certainly never a kitchen by a member of the Relais et Chateau, where there is sometimes a distance between the guest and the chef.

But La Regalido was different right from the start. The entrance is through a vine-covered arch into a tiny but exquisite garden with just enough lawn to provide an accompaniment for roses and other seasonal flowers. The swallows were busy chasing each other from tree to bush and there were a few bright umbrellas against the Arles sun.

Inside the reception area there was an immediate feeling of acceptance. Behind the small reception desk there was a bright-eyed, black-haired woman, who proved to be the wife of the inn-keeper, and in a welcome fireplace was a small fire. It so happened that there were occasional rain showers during the time I was there and the brightness and warmth of the fire was extremely welcome. There were bright flowers around this reception-lobby area and many brightly shining copper utensils on the walls, along with scenes from the local countryside, all original oils and watercolors.

Jan-Pierre spoke excellent English and we had a very lively conversation about the cuisine of the house. When I asked him whether it was classic or nouveau cuisine, he replied, "Fifty- fifty—I learned from my father who had a restaurant in Toulons and grew up in the business."

I've seen it this way in American country inns so frequently. Two people working hard and raising a family and loving their work. I wish that everyone could have seen this kitchen; it's much larger than a kitchen in an American inn and has a splendid array of pots and pans, knives, cleavers, herbs and spices, wines, and all the essentials. But so very clean. I can still remember the scent of fresh asparagus, strawberries, onions, and wonderful green lettuce with droplets of water.

The guest rooms are quite "cottagey" and have beautiful bright colors. It's really a wonderful place to wake up in the morning with the windows open to the garden; I could lie abed and look at the swooping swallows.

Distances in this part of France are not very great and it would be possible to enjoy a two- or three-night stay here at this lovely little inn and tour the nearby scenic areas such as the Camargue, the city of Arles where Van Gogh found the kind of light and atmosphere that inspired him, and even venture a day-trip to Avignon and possibly Marseille.

LA REGALIDO (Relais et Chateaux), 13990 Fontvieille. Tel.: (97) 70-17. An 11-guestroom very comfortable village inn in a pleasant town, 717 km. from Paris. Exceptional gardens. Van Gogh country. A very short drive to the nearby city of Arles. Closed Nov. 1 to Jan. 15. Lunch and dinner served. Rates: See Index.

Directions: Fontvieille is just north of Arles. La Regalido is on the main street. Detailed map 83.

RESIDENCES LE PETIT NICE, Marseille

I would take it that this hotel, being a member of Relais et Chateaux, is one of the deluxe accommodations in Marseille. I have included another in the same basic area, but probably a little less "pricey."

As shown in the sketch, it sits right on the rocky shore of the Mediterranean, looking out over the harbor past a Roman lighthouse.

Le Petit Nice has the same very elegant air and atmosphere in its public rooms that I've seen in the grand hotels in Nice. The dining room has a sweeping view of the harbor and every table is placed so that diners may enjoy the sunset and the view of the harbor lights. There are marble floors, handsome chandeliers, elegant furniture, and extremely coordinated panels of wallpaper. The lounge that precedes it is furnished ornately in a turn-of-the-century manner with a little Art Nouveau added.

I can't speak for all the guest rooms, but mine was not particularly well decorated and it had none of the extras that I had come to expect of members of the Relais et Chateaux. It was quite a contrast, for example, to La Regalido in Fontvieille, where I had spent the previous night—but that was something exceptional. (The hotel brochure, on the other hand, shows very elegant bedchambers. Perhaps I got the one that needed decorating. Unfortunately, I left too early in the morning to see others.)

The location of this hotel is indeed special and it is possible to gaze out over the sea literally for hours, watching the fascinating harbor traffic in this extremely busy French port. There are many transatlantic and Mediterranean cruise ships, fishing boats, oil tankers, almost, it seems, within touching distance.

As far as I can determine there is no other hotel in Marseille that has such an intimacy with the water.

For dinner I enjoyed the bouillabaisse, although I have learned that bouillabaisse can be exceptional in even the most humble of waterfront restaurants. I had portions of two desserts; the chocolate

mousse, a specialty of the house, was delicious to say the least, and the black currant sorbet had just the right touch of tartness about it. After dinner I wandered for a moment through the garden, which was dramatically lit by strategically placed floodlights, and stood a long time on the parapet, looking out past the lighthouse to the sea.

RESIDENCES LE PETIT NICE et Marina Maldormé (Relais et Chateaux), off Corniche J. F. Kennedy, 13007 Marseille. Tel.: (91) 52-14-39. A quiet, secluded seaside luxury hotel. Closed Jan. Conveniently located for all of the attractions, gardens, cathedrals, galleries, parks, and other Marseille attractions. Rates: See Index.

Directions: These directions also serve basically to get to Residence Bompard, which follows. I came in to Marseille on the A-7 and left it at the exit for Vieux Port. Continue to a fork in the road and follow the one of the left marked "Juliet." This leads through the tunnel and emerges on the Corniche J. F. Kennedy. Follow this road, which eventually leads into the business district, and after about a mile, during which time the sea is on the right and frustration on the left, there will be a small sign for Le Petit Nice on the right, down an alley. Turn down to the end of the alley and you'll see parking for Le Petit Nice. My suggestion is that you leave your car in the parking space and use a cab for any further driving.

LA RESIDENCE BOMPARD, Marseille

This was another good find. It was recommended to me by some people I met during the two weeks I had been traveling in France, and along with Le Petit Nice it has the symbol in *Michelin* that means "very quiet and secluded." On a hill in a pleasant little park in the residential section of the city, La Residence Bompard has a small garden and a very attractive terrace where one can enjoy the flowering plants and trees and singing birds. The bedrooms are pleasant and appropriately furnished.

Breakfast is offered, but there is no lunch or dinner. I think it would be an agreeable and less expensive alternative to Le Petit Nice, and apparently there is no parking problem. There are bungalows on the grounds that have fully equipped kitchens.

The manager recommended a bouillabaisse restaurant that has a spectacular view of the harbor and, although I did not have an evening meal, I was quite impressed with the general atmosphere. The name of this restaurant is Le Rhul and it is located at the turning point on the Corniche J. F. Kennedy.

LA RESIDENCE BOMPARD, 2 Rue des Flots Bleus, 13007 Marseille. Tel.: (91) 52-10-93. A 25-guestroom very quiet hotel, about 5 min. from the hustle and bustle of the Corniche J. F. Kennedy. Convenient to all of the Marseille attractions and activities. Rates: See Index.

Directions: Follow directions already given for Le Petit Nice but, instead of turning right at sign for Le Petit Nice on Corniche J. F. Kennedy, go just a short distance farther and look on the left for restaurant Le Rhul. Turn left and proceed up the hill; do not be dismayed because it is a very narrow street. If you get lost at the top of the hill ask a friendly passant and you will discover how close you are to La Residence Bompard.

You Are Arriving in Paris. . . .

The traveler to Paris will find it most useful to know which of the two Paris airports, Charles de Gaulle or Orly, is his destination.

CHARLES DE GAULLE: There are two terminals: Aerogare I is used for foreign airlines and Aerogare II is for Air France. Aerogare I has seven satellite buildings and passengers use moving walkways. Aeorgare II, with typical Gallic practicality, is much simpler with only a short walk between the gates and passport control.

There are no porters at French airports, but carts are available at both airports. If it is necessary to deplane at Charles de Gaulle and go to one of the two Orly terminals, Air France buses leave every thirty minutes from Gate 36. One should allow at least an hour and a half.

There are free shuttle buses between the two Charles de Gaulle terminals.

Getting to the city: Air France buses leave every twenty minutes for Porte Maillot. Other buses (350) go to Gare de L'Est, and bus (351) goes to Nation. These leave every thirty minutes, and the trip takes about an hour.

A taxi ride takes about half an hour and will run between fifteen and twenty dollars. It can be worth it if it's your first trip.

There is also a train from the Roissy-Rail Station, reached by bus from Charles de Gaulle, and it goes to Gare du Nord and the Chatelet, Luxembourg, Port Royal, and Denfert-Rochereau stations. The fare is about four dollars.

Be sure to take notice of the landmarks at the terminals so that you will recognize them upon your departure. Air France coaches leave every twenty minutes for Charles de Gaulle I and every fifteen minutes for Charles de Gaulle II. The bus terminal is in the basement of the Palais de Congrès at Porte Maillot. Allow an hour to be on the safe side.

ORLY: There are two terminals at Orly: Orly Sud (south) and Orly Ouest (west). These are connected by shuttle buses. The west terminal is used for French domestic flights; the south terminal for everything else. Use the green-light line if you have nothing to declare.

Carts, but no porters, at Orly.

Air France buses leave from Orly Sud to the Invalides Terminal every twelve minutes from Exit I. The cost is about four dollars. Bus 215 at Exit D goes to Place Denfert-Rochereau, on the south side of Paris, and costs about a dollar.

It's O.K. to take the rides that are being hawked by the free-lance taxis, but vehicles in the well-organized taxi line are supervised by the police. The cab to the Opéra from Orly Sud will run about sixteen dollars. You should figure on a ten percent tip plus the luggage cost, which is nominal.

Air France coaches to Orly Sud and Orly Ouest leave Les Invalides every ten minutes. It's a short ride by comparison, but still allow an hour.

NOTES

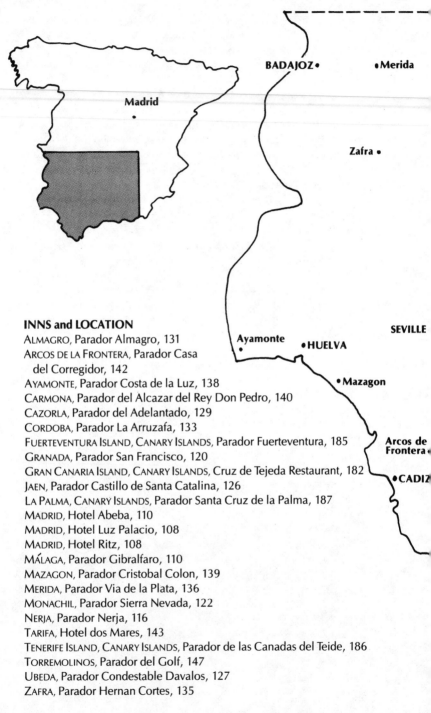

BADAJOZ •   • Merida

Madrid
•

Zafra •

SEVILLE

INNS and LOCATION

Ayamonte   • HUELVA
•

• Mazagon

Arcos de
Frontera •

• CADIZ

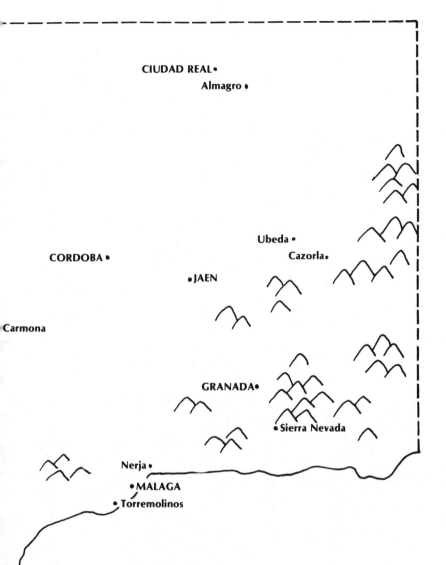

CIUDAD REAL•
Almagro •

Ubeda •
Cazorla.

CORDOBA •

•JAEN

Carmona

GRANADA•

•Sierra Nevada

Nerja •

•MALAGA
• Torremolinos

Tarifa

SPAIN
ITINERARY # 1 (Page 110)

INNS and LOCATION